CHOCOLATE THOUGHTS

*(Short Stories, Essays and Poetry
from the
Hearts and Minds of Real Black Men)*

S. JAMES GUITARD

*Literally
Speaking
Publishing
House*

*Literally Speaking Publishing House
Washington, D.C.
www.LiterallySpeaking.com*

Literally Speaking Publishing House
2020 Pennsylvania Avenue, #406, Washington, DC, 20006

ISBN: 1-929642-00-8

Library of Congress Catalog Card Number: 99-66039

Literally Speaking Publishing House hard cover printing January 2000

Printed in the U.S.A.

HALLELUJAH

**God and God alone
is worthy of all the Praise and the Glory.
Jesus Christ is Lord and Savior.**

Thank you, Jesus, for your grace. Thank You, Jesus, for your mercy. Thank you, Jesus, for teaching me that whether or not I am faced with hurt, heartache or hardship, there is always healing through your name. No matter what trials, tribulations or troubles that come my way, I must always trust you and your Word which is the Holy Bible. At times, my life will definitely be filled with moments of pain, persecution and problems, but I still have joy because I understand the power of prayer and praise. I am able through the blood of Jesus Christ to get better versus bitter when faced with life's adversity. I am unsure what type of burdens tomorrow holds, but I am certain of this: Jesus Christ would not have brought me this far to leave me now.

SPECIAL
ACKNOWLEDGEMENT

Terri Dickerson. Not only are you a dream come true, but I am deeply appreciative of all of your hard work in helping me make a dream come true. *Chocolate Thoughts* has blossomed into a much better book than I could have ever imagined since you became involved. Your willingness to endure countless hours of meetings, edits and re-edits, as well as the providing of emotional support, will not and cannot be forgotten. Since the time we met, I have been impressed, not by what you do or where you have been, but who you are: A woman of Integrity, Intelligence, Beauty, Kindness and Holy Ghost filled. God Bless and Thank You for all your love and patience.

ACKNOWLEDGEMENTS

The names of the people who contributed to the success of "Chocolate Thoughts" is a book in itself. I deeply appreciate all of those who tolerated my endless late night calls requesting that they listen to one more short story, essay or poem. In particular, I would like to thank all of the Black Men who read the writings and validated them with their lives.

Special thanks to all the Black Women who took time out of their busy schedules to read "Chocolate Thoughts." Their feedback was insightful and provocative. The "love" they have shown for the book touches my heart. I am extremely grateful for all the accolades they have given to a book that had them in mind when I created it.

Every time you are admiring the artistic quality of the book cover, think of Rod Dennis of Colabours Incorporated. Once again, thank you, Rod, for an excellent job. The book cover design receives great reviews wherever I go.

A state of the art web site design was a must. Thank you Maurice Calhoun for your visionary design. The web site is definitely award-winning.

The writing of the book was the easy part. The editing was excruciating. That is why I have saved my closing acknowledgments for the greatest thing a writer could have: great editors. My special thanks to Verna P., Verna E., Lisa, Tam, Patrice and Laurie. Stay Chocolate.

CHOCOLATE
THOUGHTS
*(Short Stories, Essays and Poetry
from the
Hearts and Minds of Real Black Men)*

CONTENTS

CHOCOLATE
THOUGHTS
(Short Stories, Essays and Poetry
from the
Hearts and Minds of Real Black Men)

CONTENTS

CHOCOLATE
THOUGHTS
*(Short Stories, Essays and Poetry
from the
Hearts and Minds of Real Black Men)*

CONTENTS

CHOCOLATE
THOUGHTS
(Short Stories, Essays and Poetry
from the
Hearts and Minds of Real Black Men)

CONTENTS

BLACK MEN

They fear my presence. My intelligence. My boldness. The quest and zest for life I bring. The conviction. Aggressiveness and sense of value and importance I have for life. My life. My people. Black people. Africans. People of African descent. They stare. Roll their eyes. Take deep breaths of dismay. Disgust. Anger. I was a trouble-maker. Rabble-rouser. A problem. A person to shun. Avoid and be stopped. I was the embodiment of all that they fear. Hate and Despise. Meek. Docile. Passive. Subservient were not me, you see, and that is why it is not meant for me to be seen nor heard. But bound and gagged in chains and manacles of oppression and discrimination. All because I want to be me.

YEAH, I KNOW WHAT I WANT

While rolling her mascara-covered eyes toward the back of her head, the smart aleck, under-employed but high class attitude waitress sighed deeply and stared as she mouthed off something about, "Aren't you ready yet?"..."Don't you know what you want?"..."Do you know what you have a taste for?" I sat in the restaurant booth. Motionless. Timeless and seemingly endless. As she turned to leave, I motioned my lips to say, "Yeah, I know what I want." Can I have some peace of mind. Happiness. Tranquillity. Serenity. Joy. Equal opportunity or any opportunity at all. Actually, I'm willing to try anything, but I've had enough Grief, Burden and Sorrow. Enough Pain, Bitterness and Suffering. Enough Broken-heartedness, Troubles, Trials and Tribulations. Enough Betrayal, Anger, and Persecution. So why don't you just serve me today's, yesterday's and tomorrow's special of "Good Times and Lots of Love and Respect" and stop telling me you're out of it, every time I ask for it.

I HAVE SOMEONE FOR YOU TO MEET

After waking up and looking over at the calendar, I knew right away that I was going to buy flowers for my wife. I just didn't know whether or not they were going to be long stemmed roses with a touch of baby's breath or a big bouquet filled with violets, tulips, carnations and at least one birds of paradise flower. So as soon as time permitted, I made a bee-line straight for the flower shop. I was determined to stop vacillating. It was my lunch hour and I was going to make a decision. Then it happened. Finally it was over. I had the flowers in my hand walking proudly up to the cashier when the sales woman approached me to tell me how beautiful the flowers I had were. But it didn't stop there. She wanted to know who was so special that I would spend so much time selecting each flower so meticulously. I was surprised by her comment but not to the extent of how surprised I was when she added that she wanted to know what type of special occasion had happened to deserve the flowers. Was it someone's birthday or was it an anniversary? Did someone receive a promotion or were they getting an award? Is there a wedding or graduation ceremony? What did I do wrong was the next question. You must have done something mighty bad to give someone flowers that looked like that was her conclusion. I stared at her and just chuckled. The answer was – none of the above. I was in love. I had the type of woman who is so special that every day she is worthy of having roses and flowers. I began telling the sales clerk how when I woke up in the morning, I had this deep felt urge to gather the most beautiful flowers man could ever find. These flowers were not only going to be for my wife, but they needed to meet my wife. These flowers had a destiny. They were the type of flowers which were used to people staring at them and telling them how beautiful they are and how they light up the room when they appear. They make people smile. Feel Happy and Loved. It was their turn now. I wanted them to feel the same level of joy that they have brought to so many people. I wanted them to meet someone who was beautiful, not only on the outside, but on the inside. And it is for that reason that I am introducing them to my wife.

DEDICATED TO YOU

A t this point in our relationship, I have come to the conclusion that the word love no longer can describe how I feel about you. The magnitude of how much I care, the intensity with which I miss you, the degree to which I want to make you happy, cannot be expressed by telling you, "I love you." The mere fact that you have heard the words "I love you" in a past relationship confirms that you will not be able to grasp how much you mean to me, when I say it. For the reality is, no man, except for Jesus Christ himself, has or will ever love you more than I do. That is why I need another word. Not just a synonym or acronym, but a powerful, potent word that makes you shiver every time you hear it. A word so filled with passion and conviction that your eyes water just in anticipation of me saying it to you. Until that day comes, it is my only hope that my everyday actions of putting these feelings into practice will make up for the inability to express them to you in words. So what I want for you to do right now is fall into my arms and allow me to squeeze you ever so carefully and sensually. Let the warmth, sincerity, tenderness and protectiveness of my arms say what man has yet to define.

I WON'T BOW DOWN

Hundreds of years of collective dehumanizing and demasculating depictions, imagery and acts. Hundreds of years of having venom, vile and rage directed, not only at me, but bred within me. Causes me to be neither sober nor distraught by the reality that there remains and will remain an insatiable desire and hunger by society to fixate itself on tormenting my life, crushing my spirit, destroying my will to live as a Black man unless I submit to a life of being impotent of courage, self-respect and dignity, while simultaneously relegating my existence to lurking in a state of ignorance, apathy and self-degradation.

YOU CAN GET ALL THE SHOES
YOU WANT

S he didn't understand why I sat so patiently, smiling in the ladies' shoe department in the middle of a busy holiday sale. But here I sat. Legs crossed. Arms sprawling. Grinning from ear to ear. Never glancing down at my watch or giving her a scowl look to indicate that I was ready to go. Because today, I was experiencing what so many brothers are missing out on. The joy that comes from being in a monogamous relationship. For the first time, I wasn't nervous or edgy about being in a department store during the holiday season. I didn't have the need to constantly look over my shoulder to see if there was another female around whom I was seeing. No need for my eyes to take a panoramic view of the store aisles in the hope that I could spot someone who would blow my cover in advance then cleverly divert them without the woman whom I was with detecting anything. My palms aren't sweaty. My mind isn't concocting alibis to match past alibis nor creating future alibis to match events that haven't even occurred. I am finally at relationship peace. Relieved. Stress free. It's almost to the point where I can do the unspeakable. Hold hands.

LIAR

T hat's why I want a divorce," and click, is all I remember from the two and a half hour shouting match my soon to be ex-wife and I had last night. So I sit in the same position in the hotel room. Staring into space. Phone still pressed to my ear. 8 hours later. The sound of the busy signal continues as my other hand grips the comforter in a balled fist. We had had many other arguments before on subjects with much more at stake and with egos more inflated. But this shouting match was different. Not because the screaming was extremely loud...because it wasn't. I can remember many an argument in which the shouting was louder. But never had a conversation seemed so spiteful. It was as though she had been preparing for this conversation for awhile. Holding her cards and the venom that spilled from her tongue until she had reached a point emotionally where she could handle the consequences. And that is why I knew early on that this was not going to be an easy conversation, but I didn't plan on it ending the way it did. There were definitely issues in which we saw things differently, but that wasn't new. We were both strong-willed and head strong, and that's part of what has made our bustling careers so successful. But the same traits which have made our careers so successful were now making the ability to resolve our relationship difficulties almost impossible. We both staked out positions that left very little room for compromise. Each person seeking often not to understand, but only to be understood. But now, all that seemed meaningless. I don't know the extent to which what she said she meant, but I know whether said in a moment of rage or not, the mere fact that it was said has altered the relationship forever. That comment alone made her a liar. For while I can't move right now, I remember when I was moved when she told me she would love me forever. And that she would never leave me, ever. And that we were meant to be together forever. And while I don't know what time it is. I know it's ever.

WITH THE WOMAN WHOM I LOVE

I 've been struggling for quite awhile with the issue of what has been the purpose of all the pain and suffering that I experienced in my past relationships. All of the broken dreams and unfulfilled promises. All of the hopes of planned futures that are now memories so hurtful that I don't even like talking about them to myself, let alone to anybody else. I've needed healing, but even with the healing process, I still have had questions of whether or not I would ever want to feel so vulnerable again, so exposed to sadness, sorrow and heartache. I've found myself at times sitting in the middle of the dark room asking myself, do I want to trust somebody or anybody with a part of me or all of me, if it means that I can possibly end up here again. Hurt, teary-eyed and still alone. For the longest, I've not had answers to these questions, but I have been content with the realization that every day is another day further from the pains of my yesterday. Then you appeared, and slowly but surely it all started to make sense. The time it has taken for us to get to know each other has been beneficial. I have grown, you have grown, and consequently we have grown. I would never have truly appreciated your thoughtfulness and considerate ways had I not had something to compare it to. I might have liked you, but I never would have been able to grasp how special and unique that you are. Most importantly, I wouldn't be as open to compromise, respectful of loyalty and commitment, or as dedicated to enjoying each and every time we laugh or share a special moment. So yes, I'm moving on and we are moving on together, but I've brought a piece of my past with me. Not to hinder us, but to propel us. For each day that I remember where I have been allows me to better appreciate where I'm at. With a woman whom I love, who loves me back.

CHOCOLATE THOUGHTS AND ALMOND QUESTIONS

It would take only one more glance at her body outlined under the bedroom sheet to know I didn't love her. Nonetheless, I still feel the need to stare at her chocolate covered, almond joy skin and reminisce about the one-time growing, blossoming relationship we once had that now appears destined for a dead-end. While feeling moved neither to cry nor frown, I still feel compelled to lay silent while capturing this seemingly defining moment in our relationship in the hopes that I might determine the authenticity of my own feelings. Was I really out of love, or had I ever been in it? Was our relationship at a turning point because the mere words I was often too quick to utter into her eyes now demanded commitment along with them? Had the sex I had wanted from her, and the love she had wanted from me, caused me to pretend that I loved her so much that I actually started to believe it myself? Was it something she did or didn't do or couldn't do or wouldn't do or was it something that I'm afraid of doing or don't want to do? These are the questions that I posed to myself over and over again as the curtain blew back and forth in the evening air. Like a gambler who never knows when to quit. Never recognizes nor treasures the benefits of what he already has. I've always thought about who's next. Whose warm thighs would curl themselves around my legs? Whose lips would ever so softly press against mine? Whose heart and soul will light up or ache at the mere mention of my name? But not tonight. Tonight, once and forever, I'm going to stare into the night and solve the mystery of why I'm never satisfied with what I have no matter how good it is or how good it wants to be to me.

PLANNED LOVE

This is exactly the way I would have planned it. The woman whom I love has tears streaming down her face with no desire to wipe them away. A 1 1/2 carat, diamond ring, Letter D, VS 1 cut, with baguettes, sits on top of her left hand for all the world to see. The emotions of the event just flabbergast us. All during last night and today I've been trying not to tip my hand. Not to say anything or do anything that would indicate that today would be one of the happiest days of my life. It's been difficult keeping the engagement plans a secret, but it is no secret to anyone who knows me or has seen us together that I am not only in love with this woman, but am dedicated to making my fiancee the happiest woman in the world. When we first met, I didn't think it was going to lead to marriage. Clearly, there was something special about her. Many people I know concentrate on her figure and overall looks. Others on how witty and graceful she is when she is in a crowd or talking to them one-on-one. I was impressed by these things, but not enough to marry her. I needed more. It may sound old fashioned, but this is what made the difference for me. I remembered reading in Proverbs 31:30 that "Charm is deceitful and beauty is passing but a woman who fears the Lord, she shall be praised." Other people may be moved or enticed by her other attributes, but I have always been struck by her desire to want to serve and live for the Lord. And yes, you are right, I am glowing, because I recognize and appreciate that I have standing before me a virtuous woman in my life whom I will continue to grow to understand is worth far more than rubies.

WHOSE FAULT IS IT

This time when I pulled out of her and removed the latex condom, it wasn't just her I was pulling out of, but the relationship as well. After a year and a half of going back and forth on this issue in my mind, I had finally concluded that after making love to her, I wasn't in love with her. That love she was so willing to receive and embrace had been delivered to her address, but if she looked ever so carefully, she would realize it didn't have her name on it. Whether it was addressed to someone who had been there before her or someone yet to come, however, seemed irrelevant to her. She opened it anyway and took all the love that was in it. So as I wrap my arms around her and she lays her head against my chest while squeezing me ever so tightly with her legs, I wonder who is more dishonest and wrong. Me, for sending her love that I know didn't belong to her, or her, for opening up love she knew wasn't hers.

I DIDN'T KNOW IT WAS GOING TO BE LIKE THIS

When I told you I wanted to marry you, I didn't know it was going to be like this, but the birth of our newborn has reinforced to me how truly blessed we are to have a such a beautiful and healthy baby. Initially, when we got married, I felt fortunate and perhaps even considered myself lucky, but I never truly felt blessed. I didn't understand the gift that God had given me by placing you in my life. I've always cared for you, but that hasn't translated into really appreciating you. But all of that is changed. I now recognize that the only possible way I could end of up with as wonderful and as beautiful as a woman that you are, is if God had opened up heaven and allowed for one of his angels to leave from the pearly gates in order for you to become my wife. So every day I will rejoice, not only for the joy of our newborn, but also for my newborn appreciation for the blessing that I get to call you my wife. My sweetheart. My soulmate.

UNFULFILLED DESIRES

The hardest thing about letting her go is knowing that I want her back. And it is there that my sorrow and agony lie, because deep down I know I've made the right decision in forcing her out of my life, even as I crave more than ever for her to return in it. For though life has shown me that the love, commitment, and support I demand, she remains incapable of giving, it hasn't stopped me from wanting the love she gives, even if it means I'll never truly be fulfilled. So at night, when my mind changes the softness of my pillow into her breast and I feel this burning urge to squeeze the pillow case ever so tightly in my arms and call her. I won't. Instead, I let the tears flow from my eyes. For I am unfulfilled whether she is here or gone.

REFLECTIONS ON MY RELATIONSHIP WITH LOVE

It hasn't been that long since I thought I would never stop missing her, but as my new relationship begins to blossom, I realize now that I was dead wrong when I thought I would never feel happiness again. The truth is, it's not her that I miss at all, but instead what she meant to me, and what conversely I meant to her as well as the role we played in each other's lives. However, through time, a new woman has started to replace many of the roles that my ex once played by carving out some new roles for herself within my life based upon the uniqueness of our new experiences together; the assets which make her special as well as the internal growth that has occurred within me since my previous relationship. So now, when I come across a photo enshrining a special time my ex and I shared, I am no longer immediately saddened. Instead, I've grown to appreciate that though those times were indeed often joyful, happy and definitely special and therefore a part of me, they are not the end of me nor my happiness. So tonight, when I look into the eyes of the woman who makes my knees quiver, heart race and lips moist, I will understand that it is not her that I am in love with-- but love itself. For I have fallen in love with the love that love brings.

HOW CAN YOU

S o I ask myself: "How do you do it?" How are you not repulsed by the evil of your deeds and the society that has been molded in your image of vulgarity? How do you, and all of your accomplices, rejoice and exalt in a society which is nauseating and detesting to God's words and teachings. What of the poisonous "Good Ole Days" makes you salivate the most. Is it the clinging of the shackles, that though not visible, still bind the majority of my brethren, or is it the cumulative effect my political and economic castration has had on the abundance of your economic prosperity? What fuels your ability, if not evil, to acquire spoils by oppression and discrimination while cloaking your transgression in the name of God and God's blessings? I ask today, tomorrow and for all yesteryears. How can you continue to promulgate the virtue of this sadistic nation while claiming that you lack duplicity for its ills when you have been the primary and almost exclusive beneficiary of its

CHOCOLATE THOUGHTS

wealth and privileges?

IT'S NOT YOURS TO SHARE

My rage and sadness are not directed at the fact that she had given him the kitty (smile) but that she gave him our cat. After years of love-making and having sex and being told that the cat was mine and all mine, I really started deep down to believe it. So even though we had recently broken up, that didn't stop me from thinking that I had the right to ask her where she was last night. When she replied "None of your business," I was hurt and felt violated. How could she give to another man, my cat, our cat, so soon? Whether she understood it or not or even cared, the reality is, I need time to emotionally withdraw from believing that I had co-ownership. I need to be able to close my eyes and clear my thoughts of any and all imagery of her giving our joy to someone else other than me. As far as I am concerned, I want it to acquire cobwebs until we get back together, if we get back together, or remain closed and unused until I no longer care who has it. For now, I seethe with anger, for whether you believed the relationship crumbled because of my shortcomings or her faults or the culmination of different factors, this remains true: Even if I didn't or don't love her, I have always loved the feeling of importance I felt when she gave and told me that the cat was mine. All mine.

IT IS HARD NOT TOO

I promised myself that the next time I was in this situation my response would be different. I would not allow myself to wrap my arms around you in such a way that would pull your body against mine. I would refuse the temptation to stare deep into your eyes and tell you how much I love you and only you, while knowing deep down in my heart that I didn't. But ever since the first time you told me that you loved me, I've felt this need to say those same words back to you even though I know they were a lie. For I just want to feel the way you say I make you feel when I say I love you. And maybe, just maybe, telling you I love you is the beginning of falling in love with you.

FINALLY

There are no balloons nor flowers to celebrate this moment. No hallmark card, laughter or applause accompanies what is truly one of the happiest moments in my life. Just unseen tears of joy. For the first time since we have been together, I can look into your eyes, and I don't see hers. When I hold your hand or squeeze you so ever so close to me, I no longer wish deep down it was her. When I pull you close and whisper how much you mean to me, I'm no longer scared that I will say her name instead of yours. I've finally closed one of the most difficult chapters in my life. The memories of the love I once shared with her no longer take precedence over the love I now share with you. The tears and joy of my past relationship no longer define the reality of what our relationship is, nor can become. Time has healed what my heart and mind could not do on it's own. So you're right when you look at me and ask me if something's wrong, because I appear to be acting weird or different. There is something different. Finally, when I say, "I love you," I mean I truly love you and only you.

TIME BOMB

There are so many deep, unresolved issues in my life. Feelings and emotions that I keep chained to a fence. Locked up. Caged tight within my heart, not because of the havoc that I fear they would wreak on the world, but the emotional insanity it would cause internally to confront them. The rage. The emptiness. The anger. The loneliness. The feelings of despair and lack of direction that encase my soul and engulf my spirit as I drift endlessly from one day to another with no purpose or focus, but a distant hope for a better day or life. Tears of sadness and disappointment spew from my heart but never reach my eyes for the world to see. To the world, I seem cold. Distant. Ruthlessly misdirected and enraged with evil intentions. An animal to be tamed. Subdued and held in captivity. Fear of the bomb that ticks in every Black man awake or a sleep, assimilated or righteously conscience, scares the general population at large as well as knowingly or unknowingly our own selves. Every moment I breathe, I hear the ticking of the bomb. The ticking of life's clock drifting away from me. Causing me to become more irrationally sane in my actions and thoughts. "Why me" is some philosophical questioning that I have given up answering. Choosing instead to devote my energies to trying to control the poison injected into my mind by hundreds of years of psychological castrations of strong Black male imagery, while simultaneously feeling the need to drink the nectar of the devil's poison in order to survive the psychological and emotional onslaught I endure in this cruel evil demonic world. Self-destructive senseless imagery occupies the thoughts of mind as I spin relentlessly in circles searching for a pathway out of my sociological enslavement and bondage. Fearful of no one but myself and what lurks within.

YOU HAD TO KNOW

I don't understand why she told me she loved me. She had to know this couldn't grow. Even before I first entered into her, I knew I would never enter into a relationship with her. So as we put back on our clothes after an evening of toe-curling, passionate sex, I find myself thinking, not about the future we won't have. but instead about the first time we ever caressed and kissed. For while that day was the beginning of our affair, it also ended any hopes of us being anything other than unfaithful. Dishonest. and Untrustworthy. That is why during the course of the last several months, I have treasured each of the stolen moments we have had. The laughter, the smiles, the pleasures have all been genuine. The fun has been and continues to be fun. We both enjoy each other's company, but the reality is, no matter how much of a good time we steal, it can't change the truth that our time together is based on deceit. So I believe the best response I can give to her telling me she loves me is to say "You are so special." This places the ball back in her court. If she chooses, she can ask me why I didn't I say, "I love you," back, or she can pretended that my words and her words are interchangeable, just as we have pretended that what we are doing isn't that bad or that there are justifiable reasons for why we permit ourselves to do something that we know is wrong and wouldn't want done to us. However she responds to what I say, I know this much, even with all of my faults and duplicity in our shared situation, I am crystal clear that I don't want the type of love she has to offer if it's the type of love that allows for her to be here.

I LOST IT ALL

Why me, why me, why the %@!$ me. Maybe they had made a mistake. I will ask them to retest me again. There had to be something wrong with the test. Maybe I will try another doctor. There it is. The problem is the doctor. The doctor I have been going to doesn't know what the %@!$ he is doing. See, I knew that %@!$ made sense. I knew I couldn't have it. Alright now. %@!$ is going to go back to normal. Tomorrow I'm gonna let another doctor give me the test and then when the results come back negative, then I will laugh about this %@!$ in the future. I was trying to do everything in my power to convince myself that I didn't have AIDS. I couldn't believe that I was caught out there. I just wanted somebody to tell me it was a big joke. A %@!$ up poor taste joke, but a joke. A joke that I should kick your %@!$ for doing, but I'm so happy that I don't have it that I just laugh the %@!$ off and tell you you better not do that %@!$ again. I would tell them, you really had me going. For now all I could do is hope that this was a dream. A bad dream. A %@!$ up dream, but nonetheless a dream. I sat in the dark. Not a single light was on in the entire house. Luther Vandross was singing "Forever, For Always for Love" on the tape cassette. There would be no more love. I had blown everything I had over some %@!$. We were scheduled to get married. The wedding was two months away. The invitations had already been sent. The wedding was going to be funky. All my friends from way back in the day were going to be there. My parents and relatives I had not even seen in years were coming. This was going to be one of those weddings that everybody was waiting for. I was successful. A college grad. I had gone to grad school, received my MBA and was making dough on Wall Street. I was street savvy, but with intelligence. The world was all mine. If the world had not gotten me now, then it would never get me. That's what I thought. If only I had not slept with another sister. I just wanted to sleep with a couple more people, because I knew that I was going to be with this girl for the rest of my life. It was going to be the same cat every day. I would love it, but I just wanted to have something just one more time. I wanted to hear another girl scream as I take her deep. Now look what I have done. I %@!$ up my entire life. I destroyed a pretty d@## perfect relationship, and for what? A lousy piece of %@!$, I didn't even give a %@!$ about I didn't know how to tell her that the wedding was off. She asked me why, and I gave her all these bull%@!$ reasons for why we couldn't get married right now. She could see through all of them. Some of them even made sense, but not for the type of love we shared. For brothers, sex and love are different. We don't see a direct correlation between the two. I loved my girl, but I just wanted to sex this girl. Now I wish I loved the way women do. I wish my love meant that I wasn't going to f#@# anybody else, because I would no longer be f#@## anybody, I would be making love. Now when it came to sex, I wish I thought like a sister. When I told her that night she started to cry and curse me out, I understood it, but I wish she wouldn't have. Her emotions were appropriate, but I wasn't looking for appropriateness, I wanted something else. I left her alone on the park bench cursing me with every word she could think of knowing in my heart that she was right for feeling that way. I couldn't stay for any more abuse, though. The burden on my own heart was already so strong that I couldn't carry anyone else's burden no matter how valid it was. I told her I wish it would have never happened and how I would re-do everything if God gives me a second chance. She heard the words, but understood, as I did, that no matter how valid what I said was, what was done was done. If I cheated on her, she would have been pissed and maybe we might have temporarily separated, but our love would have brought us back. I had gotten the one thing from which there was no return. There could be no forgiveness. There would be no happy ending. The relationship was over. I sit here now. Tears swelling up in my eyes, and I have no plans on trying to do anything to stop them from pouring out. I rock my head back and forth as the tears flush out and the emotions pour out of me. I reach out for my financial management portfolio. In the portfolio I had developed and analyzed everything in order to make our future financially secure. I had determined the future value of our stocks and bonds, the 401k plan; I had set aside money for our ranch style home; I had selected vacation destinations; I had put aside money for our children's future college education fund; I had everything mapped out. Now it was all over. I took a deep sigh that lifted up my chest cavity as I began to wipe the tears away. Page by page I began to rip and tear each single page of the 475 page financial management portfolio book into shreds. I tossed the torn pieces of paper into the garbage recognizing at that same time that by sleeping with that other sister, I had tossed my future away also. The clock on the wall continued to tick. The moon shined bright. Everything in the house appeared normal, in its right place, but here I am tearing up a book, wiping away tears, as the reality of my actions have fully set in on me. Damn, I don't know what to do.

FATHER'S DAY

This much I now know is true. If events in my life had actually happened the way in which I had planned them, then the very things that I have come to appreciate and treasure the most wouldn't exist. So, as my daughter, clad in her barrettes and shiny vaselined legs, places one of her small hands within mine, I can't help but beam with joy. For some strange reason I always pull my daughter especially close to me when we enter into the family church in which she was baptised. If you haven't already noticed, the beautiful woman at my side is my wife. Today, like every other Sunday, her ensemble is topped with one of her larger-than-life Phyllis Hyman hats, which is always tilted against the afternoon sun's glare. The word of God can be found every day, not only in the Bible she carries, but most importantly in her heart, actions and deeds. The thought, let alone the reality of my wife or daughter not being part of my life is impossible to imagine.

My wife and I have a bond that allows me to always feel her presence without ever seeing her. We can sense each other's thoughts without exchanging a single word. That is why I know today is a very special day, not only for me, but also for her, too. Father's Day is a celebration for our family of not only the Christian parent that I am, but also the God-fearing and God-loving spouse that I work hard at becoming better at every day. My wife and I have experienced a lot of ups and downs in love. We both know what it is like to give our all in relationships that we wanted to succeed only to have our individual efforts fail despite the fact that we wanted to love and to be in love. When I joined this church years ago, the last thing on my mind was being married or fatherhood. A succession of failed relationships, financial, family, work and health issues hit me so hard collectively that I had to develop a personal relationship with the one and only true God, who I already knew I should know better. My dreams. My aspirations. My way of doing things as well as the world's way of doing things always seemed to eventually conflict with God. When there was conflict between God and what I wanted, I would do whatever I thought was best, not fully understanding that since God is all-knowing and all-powerful, whatever God says in his word that is also confirmed by the Holy Spirit is best. Events in my life, no matter how hard I tried and no matter what temporary success I have had, always in the end would bring me grief. I adopted a lifestyle of seeking fulfillment in temporary pleasure, because the God-less approach I was using would not bring me the joy I wanted. My life was spiraling downward internally at a faster pace than people who knew me well saw on the outside. I was lost, and as the popular song from back in the day would say: "I was a man with no direction...with no purpose." I wanted God to fix my troubles according to my desires. I came to God, not to do His will, but to seek God's assistance in accomplishing my own. Prayer consisted of sending God my wish list. Bible-study, a continual belief in the power of Jesus Christ, a lifestyle led by the Holy Spirit, were once as foreign to me as the woman I would meet in Bible-study and later join in happy, holy matrimony. God has taught me that in order for him to have a breakthrough with a person like me, I had to have a breakdown. But now I have not only changed, but I have also grown. I understand what Hebrews 11:24 means, "By Faith Moses, when he came of age refused to be called the son of Pharoah's daughter, choosing rather to suffer affliction with the people of God than enjoy the passing pleasures of sin, esteeming the reproach of Christ greater riches than the treasures of Egypt; for he looked to the reward. By faith he forsook Egypt, not fearing the wrath of the king; for he endured as seeing Him who is invisible." So it is fitting that my daughter would whisper in my ear, "How much longer, Daddy?" I tell her "Not long, Sweetie," as I lift her head from my shoulders and transfer her to her mother's outstretched arms. "Just take a nap on Mommy's lap". Then I proceed to stand up and get ready to get my Holy Ghost sanctified shout on. With every Hallelujah and Thank You Jesus, I think of not only how blessed I am today, but also forever more, to have what I could never imagine to be so important. A clean heart. A Holy Spirit led life and family. A loving wife and beautiful daughter. Truly, my daughter will know what it is like to live in a household with a father who fears the Lord and serves God in sincerity and truth. A man who put away the gods which he onced served and now serves only the Lord. A man who is so strong in his faith, it doesn't matter to him if others feel it is evil to serve God, because he has already chosen whom he will serve. A man who will teach his child that as for me and our house, we will serve the Lord.

ASSAULT

I am so beat up, battered and assaulted. I can still feel the bruises, swelling and wounds all over my body. The pain is so excruciating, I can barely speak. I just sit in the hospital emergency room. Waiting to be seen by a medical intern, even though the type of medicine I need, I know he can't prescribe. There is no such thing as heartbreak medicine. The type of love I've come down with can't be cured with a shot. An ace bandage wrap can't heal the feeling of being used. The wasted time and love cannot be surgically restored. So I sit quietly, looking at different people faces' grimace due to their fevers, stomach ulcers and broken bones. Thinking how lucky they are, while simultaneously wishing deep down that I could somehow trade places with them.

HARD TRUTHS

I could feel the tears but I kept telling them to go away. That's what I remember most. The feeling of rejection which reminds you that the intellectual acumen of African-Americans will never be recognized for its value. No matter how much we equal or surpass whites' intellectual curiosity or attainment, we will always be the equivalent of the mathematical symbol, less than. So we relegate ourselves to a lifetime of having to be twice as smart, but never being allowed to be twice as good.

COMBAT PAY

I fell back on the couch and tried to catch my breath from another exhausting day of being Black. One deep sigh after another is all you hear in the apartment, except for the occasional hip hop music blaring music out of the trunk of a kitted down jeep zooming down the street or the "meta...meta" bongo music playing in the apartment on top of a red, yellow and green flashing light Puerto Rican bodega on the corner. Slowly I close my eyes and try to bring some form of inner peace and serenity to my soul and body that I never see in the ever-changing but racial-hatred maintaining world I call home. Being Black for me and for countless others is a job, an occupation, damn near a career, I thought as I reflected on the harsh reality of suffering and anguish that permeates itself throughout every day, hour, and minute that we Blacks find ourselves spending in a society that professes to be a melting pot of ethnic diversity but is really a caldron filled with boiling hate and divisiveness, seasoned with class inequity and intolerance. At the end of each suffocating week, being Black should entitle you to be able to go somewhere and pick up a Black survival weekly supplemental paycheck. You should be able to walk up to the cashier and tell her that today, and in general this week, has been especially unbearable, and therefore you are applying for Black overtime. She would look at the pay scale and calculate the amount of extra abuse you suffered beyond the normal everyday sorrow, suffering and injustices that you are expected to endure, because the pigmentation that God had selected for you was a dark hue. Upon her completing the necessary mathematical calculations, you would then gather your check and evaporate into an endless sea of misery and despair with at least a semi-smirk smile of gratification and recognition that being Black can be so exhausting and stressful that it is commonly understood that it merits a paycheck, no matter how small a pittance it may be. Perhaps it wouldn't be so bad if you got an occasional day off. If every once in awhile you could call in sick and say, "Hey, I'm really feeling under the weather from the racial pressure of being Black, so today I'm gonna take the day off." Remember when you see me today, no preconceptions that I'm a criminal, thief or degenerate to society. No relegating my existence on this planet to that of sub-human inferiority level in order to support your false sense of racial superiority and dominance. No, today we are all going to interact as the God giving life to human beings of equal chromosome level that he intended us to be. If we can't have that, maybe we could take shifts during the day. During the day I would punch in and out of my "Black, I'm supposed to get abused card" in order to indicate the hours I have worked. When confronted with one of the multiple daily indignities and confrontations, I would pull out my card and say "Hey, I'm off duty," and then proceed to receive the fair, just and equal treatment that always seems to evade Blacks no matter how much we relentlessly pursue it. If that wasn't satisfactory, maybe the world could provide annual gift certificates to those of us who survive and endure the endless onslaught of racial hatred and discrimination without spiraling downward into an empty abyss of alcoholism, drug addiction and spiritual decay. For now, all I can do is take a deep breath and hope with each one that my soul and spirit are released of their surmounting and ever present stress and pressure of being Black in a world conquered, controlled and dominated by whites bent on subjugating me because of my skin.

CLEANSING WITHOUT REDEMPTION

The sanitizing of racism is white America's panacea for its unwillingness to grapple with the dehumanizing torment racism has had on the psychological, social and economic and political well-being of African-Americans. Therefore, when white society is confronted about its unquestionable blatant acts of individual and institutional racism, they are less likely in the 21st century to pretend to be aghast by its existence, but instead are choosing to disavow the contention that their hideous acts of racism are indeed racist or even have racial undertones. This self-imposed amnesia concerning the historical and contemporary oppression of African-Americans is necessary in order to maintain the illusion of equal opportunity and justice for all; even though an overwhelming abundance of empirical and anecdotal evidence would refute that such opportunity exists. The revision of African-American suffrage, redefining of racism and civil rights as well as the disavowing of

73

progressive voices in the Black community, are all necessary if white society is to divulge themselves from the incivility of their amoral acts without repenting for their horrendous atrocities.

DAMN IT'S COLD OUT HERE

Sometimes I can feel the chill cutting down my spine causing my teeth to chatter. I wanna place my balled fist deep in my pockets, tuck my head as low as I can into the shoulders off my neck, in order that I may be able to somehow avoid the impeding cold that is gushing around in this icy cold world. Head low and pushing forward, that's me. Deep breaths of concentration consume my mind as I concentrate on better days. It has got to get better. It can't go on like this. Nobody should have to live like this. Nobody should have to endure the level of hate, scorn and contempt that is directed at my skin. I often find myself asking what is it about this Black skin. This chocolate. Brown sugar. Caramel. Coca complexion that drives so many people who even look like me to hate it. I stare at myself in the mirror. Trying to concoct images of pride and privilege in a skin complexion in order to combat the vile demonic images of demoralization and negativity that my skin represents in a

75

society obsessed with my abuse, destruction and de-masculinization. My heart often fills up with sadness and disgust that the world never sees. It hurts every time I look into a face of some nappy-haired or permed Black person with a broader nose and lip than my own, whose ancestral lineage is intricately linked to the brutal savagery of slavery that our ancestors mutually endured, who nonetheless finds it their duty and primary responsibility in life to enact moats of treason and erect stumbling blocks of treachery as they conceive, develop and implement countless obstacles to thwart my, and every other black person's, every move or goal of getting a little bit of joy and happiness before their cells incinerate into this cold, demonic-possessed world. Let alone you have some Black people whose primary claim to fame, knowledgeable or not, is based primarily on the fact that some white person spread the chocolate covered m&m legs of some Black sister as they thrust their mythological concocted superior sperm into the uninviting warmth of some Nubian queen's thighs. Nonetheless, centuries after the beastly rapes that created many light skinned Blacks, there all too often too many who still embody the false preconception that slave master's blood and semen endow them with a special rank and privilege to bestow upon the darker creed of their race; pompous, smug airs of superiority, which in folds means disdain, ridicule and contempt for all of us whose immediate family members haven't had that privilege of looking more like the slave master, i.e. the oppressor. I watch dumbfounded as every day the oppressor lures individuals willingly and unwillingly to participate in self-inflicted genocide, induced by a racial self-hating, psychological crucifixion of one's own imagery as a perquisite to receiving perceived, but not guaranteed, rainbow-in-the-sky pots of gold. Too many of us seek solace from the psychological torment of addressing the seemingly insurmountable odds of overcoming bigotry and racism by claiming to understand the imaginary incivility of our race. In so doing, we justify the subjugation and conquistadorish enslavement of the economic, social, educational, and political well being of countless and untold generations of African lineage.

FIRST LOVE

Why, after all these years, do I want to return to the rooftop in which I lost my virginity, is a question I don't fully have the answer for. But here I am, staring into the night, while inhaling the project air and all of its misery and laughter, troubles and dreams, tears and hope. Trying to find a meaning to life. My life, and more importantly, how do I improve on where I am at. Right now, all I allow my mind to think of, besides the feeling of nostalgia which makes my body shiver, is where did or does time go, and how did I let it get so far away from so quick. A mischievous grin cuts across my face. To this day, I can still feel the palm of her hands planted on my chest. Ready to push me away, but wanting to pull me closer, as her eyes plead for me to go slower since this her first time, too, and its hurts. With each pelvic thrust, tears fill her eyes as she asks me if it's good? Am I doing it right? And most importantly, do I love her and only her? I've never been able

79

to give someone the amount of love-her tears, actions and words meant in retrospect-to both of us, but I realize now more than ever that's how I want to be loved again. For now, all I can do is reflect back to days when I thought tomorrow would be a better day and hope that someone or something brings joy in my life the way she once wanted to bring.

IT'S ALL FOR THE BEST

Without warning, tears would fill my eyes and fall down my cheek, but I wasn't surprised, because I knew why they were there. Instead, I remained still and continued to stare at the empty pillowcase beside me. For I have grown to understand that wiping away the tears won't stop the pain. I have to let it flow, just as I had to let her go. So silently, I wait. Teary-eyed. For the day when my bed is filled, not just with a body, but someone who loves me.

CONSCIENCE

Terrified by my ineptitude to transcend my economic malaise, I seek solace in the warmth of a Black woman's thighs. Comforted by the sweetness of her African dessert, I gain self-importance and power, often never achieved in the world, but embodied in her eyes and her willingness to bestow upon me her Nestle Crunch treasure. How many Almond Joy, Reese Pieces, Milkway, Snicker Bars do I have to have in order to subdue the feeling of inadequacy and demasculinization thrusted on me by the world when my actions inflict pain on countless sisters' hearts trying to weave and knit their own existence together in a world submerged and entrenched in racism, classism and sexism. In my feeble attempt to find and shelter my own peace of mind, I decimate the emotional fragility of untold Black women's lives into broken fragments of used and betrayed love. After temporarily being fulfilled by sexual conquest, I seek new coconut oil-skinned prey to feed my appetite for self-esteem and personal gratification while conveniently absolving my conscience from the psychological burden of the degrading, dehumanizing torment my libido-centered outlook of life has caused.

ATTENTION NASA, TAKE OFF HAS BEEN DENIED

ow I wanted to give all the pleasure back, or at least that pleasurable day that had brought me to this point. I just stared. Motionless. Expressionless. A vacant look covered my entire face. All I could do was make eye contact. She was talking to me, but I couldn't make out all the words. She was speaking English, but my brain wasn't deciphering everything. I was getting fragments. Bits and Pieces. The only word my brain heard and kept repeating to itself was pregnant. PREGNant. pregNANT. preGNAnt. PREGNANT. "Oh-%#@$ "What am I gonna do?" I said to myself as if to alert my brain to start developing a plan. This was real. So many other brothers had been in these shoes. Now it was my turn. I listened calmly to everything she had to say. A few minutes earlier I was out of control. "D##%, %#@$, I can't believe this %#@$ I shouted at the world and at her. Why I didn't believe, I don't know.

85

She and I both didn't use protection. I had placed my %#@$ in the %#@$. Why was I shocked? I'll tell you why...because it was me. I felt I was special. I could beat the odds. I had beat the odds so far, I thought. I was immune. I was on a winning streak that would never end. I had never gotten a girl pregnant before, and this was because it was meant for me to f#@$, f#@$ well and f#@$ often. The rubber on condoms interferes with the sexual pleasure is, what I had rationalized for why I didn't wear them. I'm not gonna get caught out there. The hell with the chances of catching AIDS, HERPES, GONORRHEA, SYPHILIS, CRABS. This was me. I was mad at her. I was mad at myself. I was just mad. In the beginning, I threw things and hit walls as I cursed up a storm. The time for that was over. I was now listening to her talk about her feelings. She has tears in her eyes. In the midst of my rage she had either cried or was about to begin. "Be cool, Be cool," Cut that out I said as though I was the model for what being cool in such a situation was. "Talk to me, Babe," I said. She began to talk, and I pretended to listen. She was pouring out her heart and feeling. I tried to give the impression that I cared, but right now I didn't give a %#@$. It was my life that I was concerned about. It was my future that I was thinking about. Occasionally I would give a nod in order to indicate that I was concerned and had been paying attention. I wanted an abortion, but I didn't know if this was the time to say it. I didn't want to say something with bad timing that would cut off the communication flow and prohibit me from influencing whether she continued the pregnancy or not. You know, I always hear Pro-Choice people talk about the right of a woman to choose whether or not to have a baby. I agree that abortion should be legal, but now another question has entered my mind. I never hear people talk about the man's right to have a say about whether a woman bears a child or not. Don't dismiss what I am saying, because I am dead serious. If this woman decides to keep the baby against my wishes, then my life will forever be changed. I am either forced into a role that I don't want to play, or I have to force myself to deny the existence of the role that I know I should play. There are those who will say I brought it on myself. They are right on one part and wrong on the other. Having sex has brought me to where I am now, but there are options. Some women think that the only way they can have you or keep a man is to bear his child. That %#@$ almost never works, but women still do that %#@$ all the time. It just makes the majority of us resentful. It was too early to determine whether or not I would be resentful, but it wasn't too early for me to become suspicious of her pregnancy. "How do I know it's mine?" I asked myself, as if I were two people and the other half would provide a response. How do I know she wasn't %#@$ somebody else? She could have been giving up the p#@$ to somebody else, but wanted to claim me as the father. Sure, she didn't look the type to go out like that, but that doesn't mean she wasn't living that. She was under suspicion, and I was suspicious. She hadn't done anything detectable to imply she was seeing somebody else, but that wasn't why I was suspicious. I had never caught her with anyone or suspected she was seeing someone, but that wasn't why I was suspicious. I was suspicious because of what I had done and was capable of doing. Nothing generates greater suspicion than personal guilt. I knew I had slept with one woman while dating another, why couldn't she have done the same? She could have giving up the %#@$ to a past boyfriend or somebody who she had a crush on. I had done it; why couldn't she? That's why I don't trust nobody. I just distrust people at different levels. Life has taught me that trust comes rare and slim. I didn't distrust her, but that doesn't say how much I did trust her. I tell you what I trust. I trust that blood test we are going to have to determine who is the father of the child, or better yet, whether or not I am the father of the child. She was staring at me. Waiting for a response. A word. A hug. A smile. Something. Anything. I nodded my head up and down as though I was agreeing with something she was saying even though she had already stopped talking. "What do you wanna do?" I asked sternly as my eyebrows cut down and my jaw locked. She burst into tears. I had given her the wrong response. She had wanted a sign of love. A feeling of concern. Now was not the time for that, or at least that is what I had in my mind. This is business, not love. Whether I care for her or not is irrelevant, because right now I care about me more. I could have been more sympathetic or caring, but I wanted to get my point across. I want an abortion. I don't want to be a father, a dad, a pop. None of that %#@$. Not now. "Get away from me...I can't stand you...I hate you...You don't care about me," she said as she strung all the words together between sniffling and wiping away tears. "%#@$ that What are you going to do?" I said as if as I was getting ready to go upside that head. "Whats up?" I added for effect. "What do you mean, what's up," she yelled at me. "You know what the %#@$ I'm talking about. Don't play dumb," I said as though I didn't have time for no games. "I don't wanna talk to you...Just get away from me," she screamed at the top of her lungs as she backed away from me. I got ready to say, "F#@$ you, b#@$," but then I paused. I didn't want to cut off communications. I wasn't trying to run from my responsibility as other brothers had, including my father. Wherever the %#@$ he is. I just don't want a kid right now. I want to cool out. I want to have fun with the fellas. Once I have a kid, it's all over. I should say if I play the proper role, it's all gonna be over. There's baby food. There's diapers. There's clothes. There's hospital bills. There's this. There's that. There's just to much %#@$. Too much money. Too much responsibility. Just too. Right now she feels I'm deserting her. Maybe I am, maybe I'm not. I want her to have an abortion, I know that. I knew she and her girlfriends were going to get together and talk about me like a dog and tell her how much she didn't need me; how I'm not worth nothing and never was and all that other type of %#@$. They will say, "I got your back, girlfriend. We will work this out together. I will go to the clinic with you, or I will help you girlfriend, if you want to keep the child. " I know they be saying some %#@$ like that. I look at her from afar as she continues to cry and walk away. I wait a few seconds that seem like minutes before I start to run after her. All I could think of is D@## this f#@$ is f#@$ up. D##@. D##@. D##@.

FIRST STEPS

He looks so cute, sucking on that baby bottle. Look at him dressed in all blue with a little dab of white. Daamnn, I didn't even know they made Nikes that small. Go on with your bad self. You ain't no joke, gripping that baby bottle like that. Those are basketball hands you got right there. Those are basketball hands if I ever saw any. I loves you. I love you to death. You're my little brother, and I loves you like love itself. That's right, cuddle up in your crib. Tug on that blanket. Wrap it around you. You want that rattle? You want that rattle over there? Here it is. I'll even place it your hand. Anything else you want. Tell me. I know you can't talk yet, just point. Make eye contact. Just do something. Anything. Just give me a clue. I'll get it for you. Enjoy yourself. Lay back and relax. Suck to your heart's content. Life ain't touched you yet, so enjoy. Enjoy. Enjoy. If only life for me could be that simple. It's a whole nother story over here. That's why I want you to enjoy yourself. I don't want you to have a worry in this world right now. The world will give you enough to worry about later. Right now, you don't have the faintest idea what it is to be a Black man, a Black boy, a Black teenager, Black. You have yet to experience a woman pulling her purse closer to her body because she saw you walking down the street. You don't know how it is to see a store owner rush to lock his door and place a "closed" sign in the window just because you were getting ready to enter. Oh-yeah, life has some treats in store for you. I can't wait to see the expression on your face when a cop slams you against a wall for no reason at all and asks you to empty your pockets in search of drugs, or the time a cop pulls you over to ask for your driver's license, registration and insurance, because he wanted to make sure that fancy car you was driving wasn't stolen, as if no Blacks have enough money to buy an expensive car. Oh you're gonna think life is nothing but fun the first time you dive to the floor or run during a drive-by shooting. Let me help you with your spelling now. Can you spell J-A-I-L? Can you spell

P-R-I-S-O-N? How about D-O-P-E, C-R-A-C-K, G-U-N-S, P-O-L-I-C-E B-R-U-T-A-L-I-T-Y, U-N-E-M-P-L-O-Y-M-E-N-T, R-A-C-I-S-M?

I NOW LOVE-LOVE

I didn't know what love was or is until I tried to give it to someone, and they abused it. From that moment on, I've looked back with regret at all the squandered opportunities I've had to receive love and be in love, but didn't, due to my inability to either comprehend or grasp the magnitude of emotions and sacrifice it takes not only to give of oneself, but to expose oneself to the vulnerability of Pain, Heartbreak and Self-Doubt. So now when I think back on the tears of frustration that streamed down the faces of several Black women in my life, I recognize that their tears weren't only caused by my lack of sensitivity and attentiveness, but by the joy I was depriving us both.

I CAN SEE RIGHT THROUGH YOU

hen I look into their eyes, I can see the deep seated evil, hatred and soulless bodies of dark insidious destruction, infested with vile imageries of racial genocidal conquest and domination. A pasted smile conceived by deception and guile illuminates their faces, while lurking within exists a shallow pre-Neanderthal mind bent on spreading and indoctrinating willing and unsuspecting minds with divisiveness, distrust and discord. Demonic evil consumes their interactions with people of color while propagandizing and bastardizing Christian principles in order to accumulate untold and unseen materialistic acquisition. How can creations of God forgo all the underpinnings of humanity without being besieged by a morally correcting avalanche of guilt and restitution? Unless their existence and relationship with God is predicated on an ill-conceived notion that God's reign is a mere fictitious anecdote conceptualized by man to justify and cloak one's ideological beliefs, wants and desires.

HE IS A PART OF ME

O nce again, I find myself sitting near my CD player for several hours performing what now has become a ritual. Mourning the tragic death of another gifted and talented Black male's life that has ended suddenly. Throughout the evening, I've been fighting back emotions of grief and sorrow for this brother whom I've never met, but who seems to understand me. Song after song I listen to. One after another from his multiple CDs, before it dawns on me why I am so touched by his music. It wasn't the booming soundtrack or samples, though they are crazy hype. It wasn't his emphasis on materialism, drugs, violence or sex that often highlighted many of his popular songs, but it was his ability to make his voice heard. In a world in which my feelings, emotions, words, thoughts and struggles are muted, he had the courage, the dream and the fortitude to find a way to make money and tell it like he saw it. Unfortunately, the world he depicted on records is eerily similar to the way so many brothers see the world, but the magnitude of his message is not limited to that despair. As repugnant as I feel many of his lyrics are, I clearly understand the rationale from which they emanate. So I am caught in several paradoxes. I mourn his death but understand why he chose, as so many other brothers do, a lifestyle which is almost destined to end in agony. But if pain. Suffering. Hardship and misery is about all you know, then almost any doorway you choose to use to escape seems rational even if the joy, happiness and pleasure are short-lived and followed with grief, heartache, sorrow and possibly violent death. You can almost rationalize your behavior on the premise of two facts. One is trouble, poverty and hardship are already here and don't seem to be going anywhere. And two, death is a guarantee regardless of what you do. So why not, it would seem, get as much happiness as possible any which way you can, because in the end it can't be an worse than it is or it appears to be. At least that's what you think at the time. However, the eventuality of jail or a violent death makes the choices you have made and the demons that now haunt you worse than the suffering you had previously endured. So while I feel compelled to celebrate and exalt his determination, perseverance and resolve to succeed, I am concerned that many Black males will not reflect his tenacity to achieve, but will romanticize the way in which he achieved it and the goals for which he appeared to strive. But for now, all of this is forgotten. All I want to do is vibe to the beat. Hear him flow. And listen as he tells it as he sees it.

THERE WILL BE A PRICE TO PAY

After all we have been through or been told individually or collectively as a community, how can we not understand that many of our lives, lifestyles, dreams and aspirations are becoming further distant from God's words and teachings. Am I sacrilegious and worthy of contempt since I have never felt the burning sensation or psychological anguish of having a slave welt sculptured in my back to utter the words that proceed? Am I placing myself in a precarious position worthy of disdain and scorn when I suggest, without ever having experienced indentured servitude or ever having had sweat and tears stream down my face in a sun-drenched, sun-torched field, that we may have come to a point at which slavery and segregation were better for us than what we have now? Could the relationship an individual or a community has developed with God during times of massive oppression and subjugation be more beneficial for salvation than the

Godless direction growing numbers in our community have adopted due to the availability of wealth and materialistic prosperity? I submit to you that the idolatrous lifestyle of worshipping money and power, as well as the trappings that come along with it, place our community in a more perilous situation than even bondage, segregation and discrimination. I do not endorse poverty as a goal or living in oppression as joyful, I merely am attempting to convey that the more you feel you need God in your life, the more attentive you are to His Laws and Commandments. It appears that the more our community mirrors mainstream culture and its anti-God values and practices, the further we distance ourselves from the grace and protection of God that has brought us out of slavery and certain forms of segregation and discrimination. What good is it for a community which has received the brunt of oppression to embody the goals, values and means of achieving goals in the same manner in which the oppressor has oppressed them? Surely there must be a hefty price our community will pay that will dwarf what we currently endure in the form of discrimination and self-hate.

LOCKDOWN

The handcuffs were so tight around my wrist I could feel the metal digging into my skin. I kept my head down so no one could see me. I didn't want anybody I knew or basically anyone to see me in the back of a police car riding downtown to be booked. It wasn't the arrest that bothered me, but the fact that I didn't want to be seen as a criminal. As the car was zooming downtown, I would occasionally glance up to see if I recognized anyone on the streets as I prepared myself mentally for my first arrest. At this particular moment, nothing seemed real to me. I thought it was a dream, and very shortly I would wake up sweating in bed under the covers saying "D### that s@$&# felt real." When we got to the police station, I took one last sigh inside the car and said to myself, "Here we go." We entered into the police station from its garage. The cop hit a button on the side of an outside door, and then we were in. The door swung closed behind us, and I could hear the clicking noise of the lock. He passed off his gun, and then we went through a second door that led to the main booking room as well as the location for the holding pen. When that door closed, it was as if I could hear a thousand clicks. It felt as if an eternity of locks where being electronically bolted. As we were walking to a cubby in a room where I would be processed, all I could hear in my ears were locks going click, click, click, click, click, click. He sat me down in a chair and left the room. I leaned back on one shoulder with one leg bent and the other stretching out as I checked out the scene. I squinted my eyes and stretched my neck as I tried to see what was occurring in the corridors. I could see a brother sweeping the floor with a broom in an shiny orange jump suit with the word "Jail" spread across his back. I could hear one brother on the phone begging somebody to come down and get him out of jail before he cracked up. Another brother was speaking to the magistrate through a plexi-plastic bullet proof thick window about his bond and whether she could lower it a tad bit because he didn't have that type of money.

A bunch of brothers who were in the process of being transferred from one prison to the next were shackled together by hands and ankles. You could hear the chains rattling on the floor as they tried to move in uni-step. Brothers, Brothers, Brothers and more Brothers is all I saw everywhere. Nothing but brothers. The only place I can think of where you would see so many brothers would either be at the basketball court on a semi-hot summer day when the sun is going down or at a Minster Louis Farrakhan Nation of Islam rally. A cop came back and asked me a slew of questions from how old I was, where did I live, etc. I started to tell him that a mistake had been made. That there was a misunderstanding but that I really didn't do anything and anything, I did do, I did in self-defense. The cop never lifted his head to acknowledge what I had said, he just kept on writing. He then asked me a few more questions. What I said had meant nothing. As far as I could tell he pretended I had not even spoken. He was just going through the motions and I was just another N#%@$ getting arrested tonight to go with the N#%@$ who will get arrested later on tonight, the N#%@$

who got arrested yesterday and the day before and the day before that and the day before that, let alone the N#%@$ who were going to get arrested tomorrow. This was just another day at work of locking N#%@$ up. He was totally immune to my innocence or my guilt. I decided to stop trying to explain my situation since he wasn't paying me any mind anyway. I answered the questions that he asked me so that he could go about the business of processing the next N#%@$ after me that had gotten locked up tonight. The cop took me into the hallway and told me stay still as he took the papers he had just filled out to the magistrate. I said yeah, with a smirk, knowing damn well the cop knew I had no option but to stand there. The magistrate read my papers then motioned me to come to the bullet proof glass. I stepped up to the window, looked her in her brown eyes and said, "D### this is #%@$ up" to myself. Here was this fine brown sugar, chocolate sister looking at me and asking me if there was anything I wanted to say before she set bond for me. I gave her the best rap I could muster about what type of brother I was and where my head was at and that I had a future and didn't think I would end up behind bars. The fact is, one out of every four brothers are either in jail, prison, parole or on probation. In my community that figure even seems too low. Matter fact, that number doesn't even count the amount of N#%@$ who are arrested but are not sentenced for committing a crime. Nonetheless, I spoke to her about how shocked I was about finding myself in this position. The bottom line, when all was said and done, was that I was telling her to look out. She looked at me and believed me, or thought I told a good enough lie, or maybe it was something else that triggered in her mind as she gave me the lowest possible bond I could receive. I said thanks and asked her if she would tell the girl who was waiting for me what my bail would be. In the meantime the officer took me into a room and told me to strip. Get butt naked. Spread my legs. Lift up my balls. Let go of my balls. Wiggle my toes. Squat down. Grip my butt cheeks and spread them wide. Cough. Cough again. Cough louder. Open my mouth. Raise my tongue. Close my mouth. Put on these correction issued clothes and follow me. The officer then took me over to the holding cell.

Took off the cuffs, and I walked in. The door went "slam." There were no bars. It was a crazy thick steel tank door that shut. There was a sliding peephole up top for the guards to look over if they needed to see you. The width of the room equaled my arm span with my fingers stretched out. There was a long aluminum bench nailed to the floor. A toilet sat in the back of the cell with every fungus you could think of crawling over it. There was vomit, shit smeared into the toilet seat and piss sprayed all over the floor. A light bulb hung from the ceiling which I could picture many a N#%@$ dangling on. I was by myself, which was real cool, because all during this initial process I had been able to keep my cool. I was now in the process of waiting for my phone call and just cooling out. "This is some #%@#," is what I keep repeating to myself. Psychologically, I have already juiced myself up to the point that if somebody is placed in my cell and they even look at me wrong, then I'm f%@ them up. If they ask me what I'm in for, I'm #%@$ them up. If he moves to close in my air space, I'm #%@$ him up. Anything that could even lead one in the direction to think about trying to play me for a sucker, then I'm #%@$ him up. I don't expect to be in here long, but I can't take no chances. If there is a mistake in my records or some other wild #%@$ goes down, then I have to prepare myself mentally for that. The first step is making sure that anybody who comes in contact with me understands that any violation, no matter what type, will be dealt with the heaviest penalty. There are no exceptions and no apologies. There is only an #%@$-whipping. They let me make my phone call, so I contact a bail bondsman off a list that they have posted on the wall and ask if they would send someone down to bail me out. They tell me I need 10% of the bond and that it is not refundable. Eventually, a cop tells me to get off the phone and a guard takes me back to the holding cell. I'm standing in the cell with no watch and it seems as if I have been in jail forever. I wonder what the #%@$ is taking her so long to get the dough in order that I can get the #%@$ out of here. If that #%@$ tried to play me out, I will cold #%@$ her up so bad it would be ridiculous. I called her a #%@$ mentally but in my heart I knew she was a together sister who didn't merit being referenced in that way. She was one of the best things to happen to me. We didn't have a future together and both of us knew it, but there was a special bond, and we each gave the other something the other needed to make it to the next stage in life. I took some deep breaths and caught myself as I felt myself almost falling asleep. I start to wonder could my whole life have been a dream and could I have been locked up for a long time and could my mind have faked the story of someone coming to get me in order that I didn't lose my sanity. I start to search for clues that would prove to myself that my life as I knew it wasn't a dream. I hear screams and banging. The screams become louder and louder and then there is no noise. If that's the way it is, that's the way it is. I can't help you, I thought. You on your own troop, I wish you the best. I hear a noise at the door of the cell. The door opens up and the guard places this drunken white boy in my cell. He looked about in his 30s. He was what we call pwt–poor white trash. The cell door slammed locked. I look him dead in the eye looking for the slightest reason to #%@$ him up. I'm waiting for him to just open his mouth so I can bum rush him with a flurry of blows. He sits down on the bench in the far corner near all of the urine. I put my back up against the wall and constantly stare at him. I never take my eyes off him for one second. Looking for anything that could mean that he wants to start something off. Finally after a couple of more hours the door opens again and the guard says, "Someone is here to post your bond." I step out the cell and walk over to where the bulletproof glass is and wait to be processed again. The bail bondsman raps to me about the rules of being out on bond. I hear the bail bondsman's rap as I continue to nod my head about the things that I will and will not do. I agree to all the terms. I would have agreed to practically anything. I sign some documents here and there. The bail bondsman then snaps some photos of me. They buzz me through a door and as the door behind me closes they buzz me through another door. The bail bondsman takes a couple of photos of different profiles of me. The flashbulb flashes in my face as I turn left and right depending on which way he tells me to face. I get back all my personal belongings, and then I'm ghost. When I finally get outside and we start walking to the car, all of these emotional feelings start been activated in my body. I keep my cool as we get to the car and pull away. As she's driving, my head is bent down into my lap in the palms on my hands, and I'm taking crazy deep breaths. I have all of this emotion built up in me that I had to displace because of the environment that I was in that is now gushing out. I don't know what else I can tell you about my experience except that it made me more of Black man than I was. I now had a new bond with a new set of brothers who had themselves been locked up or arrested. There are times to this day that I think back about the experience, and though I can't remember many of the brothers' faces, I know some of them are probably still locked down and if not them, then there is another brother in that cell. That night, I was that brother.

REVOLUTION IS BETWEEN APATHY BOULEVARD AND COMPLACENCY STREET

You ain't saying anything, but you think you're doing something. You just faking the funk. It's not real. Your intentions are real. At least most of the time I believe they are. There are times when I hold you suspect. I think you use symbolic gestures to replace substance. I was driving down Martin Luther King Jr. Blvd. On my left was Frederick Douglas public housing unit. I made a right turn near Mary McLeod Bethune High school and saw a sign that said Malcolm X Community Center two blocks away. At the intersection I made a left on W.E.B. DuBois Lane, which cuts across Medgar Evers Street. I was temporarily confused on whether I should stay on W.E.B. DuBois Lane because I knew the traffic was bad due to the construction on Marcus Garvey Avenue. Graffiti all over the walls. Trash cans empty. Streets full of litter. Beer cans over here. Forty ounce

119

bottles over there. Dirt everywhere. Drug dealers on one side of the curb. Future hookers on the other. Lots of kids. No fathers. School day, but no school books. Computer games, but can't compute math. Arcade skills, but no computer skills. Urine in the air. Crack viles on the floor. People always wanting to read you about something you did or didn't do, but don't read. We need blunt talk about what's wrong in our community as well as what we need and must do, but many instead choose just to smoke blunts. Designer jeans, sneakers, coats and hats are worn by everybody, but nobody is designing a plan to change the misery and despair they live in. I shouldn't say nobody, just not enough bodies. I wonder if we will ever embody the convictions, values and self-determination that the individuals whose names appear on the street signs possessed. Would we, as individuals and a people, once and for all say "Enough is enough?" We have got to do better for ourselves, because there is no help coming but from ourselves. At least no help that doesn't have strings attached. We have all these streets, avenues and buildings named after people of African descent who have made significant contributions to addressing the political, social, educational and economic issues afflicting people of African, descent and what are we doing to live up to their names: Nothing. Nothing always seem so harsh, because somebody is always doing something. As people, collectively, we are just wasting time as our conditions get worse and remedies to fix them become harder to address. There is no reason for the power structure at-large to feel threatened by the streets, avenues and buildings named in honor of Black people, because as long as we don't embody the philosophy that they held, they are only that: streets, avenues and buildings. They are not signs of self-determination and empowerment until the actions of the individuals reflect the philosophy of the people after whom the streets, building, and parks were named. As soon as Black people think like the people for whom the buildings, etc. were named, watch how quickly those street signs and building names come down. As of now, they are symbolism without substance. Created by people who often truly believe in the vision of the individual after who the avenue, etc. is named. Unfortunately, the masses do not partake in their liberating vision of empowerment. We have to make a better correlation between the two. Our future depends on it. Today depends on it. Hell, yesterday depended on it. D###, I missed the turn for the Sojourner Truth Parkway.

DO NOT LET THE REFLECTIONS BE REAL

After another hard day of frustration and anger, I find myself at home staring at my reflection in the bathroom mirror. Black. Tired and Determined. I reach for a washcloth in the hopes that I can scrub away the disappointment and sadness that appears on my face. With each wring of the damp cloth, I try not only to rid its excess water but the feelings of inadequacy that have plagued my life. Suddenly, but not startling, I'm confronted with one of life's hardest and saddest truths to accept as a Black man. With half a smirk and sigh, I've come to realize that the bulk of the misery as well as majority of evil deeds committed against me will be done by a Black person. If I'm murdered, a Black person is more likely to have killed me. If my wife, sister or loved one is raped, a Black person most likely violated them. If I'm robbed, a Black person probably stole from me. This doesn't absolve white society from all

Heinous atrocities that they have committed nor the evil deeds they still try to achieve, but it places progressive thinking Black people such as myself with a paradox. The community that provides Black caring love that shelters me through storms of adversity is the same community that has people who look like me and cause the bulk of my everyday woes.

I DON'T HAVE ANYTHING

Every time I am leaving a department store I get this strange feeling that metal detectors are going to go off. So as soon as I make eye contact with them, I begin to slow down. I don't want to appear to be going too fast through them because then I know what they're going to say: "You were trying to run away." "You Thief." "You Liar." Regardless of the fact that I have purchased the items in my bag. Receipts in my pocket. I still walk slow. In the hopes that the pace of my walk will lessen the probability of the detectors ringing like a mad man. Causing heads to turn from every direction. It is to the point where I feel nervous or awkward every time I leave a store without purchasing something. I feel eyes all over me. Staring at me. Searching me. Probing me. Trying to determine whether or not I was that fast of a thief or criminal that they couldn't catch me stealing anything. Surely I must have stolen something. It has even gotten to the ridiculous point where I start to ask

CHOCOLATE THOUGHTS

myself, did I steal something?

NO, I DON'T WORK HERE

As a Black man, every time I'm wearing a suit in a department store, somebody walks up to me for information on how to get somewhere in the store or to show them certain merchandise. It seems that when a Black man has on a suit in a store, White people in particular will always ask if you work there and can you help them. Sometimes that just bugs me the hell on out. I'm just minding my own business, trying to do a little shopping here and there, and 50 million White people walk up to me and start asking me directions or for assistance. Some people don't even ask if you work there, they just walk straight up to you and say I need for you to show me X, Y and Z. As a Black man you always put this silly grin on your face and say, "Sorry I don't work here," and accept their half-backed apology as your fake grin says for the 99 millionth time, "No, I'm not offended." It doesn't make a d$%@ bit of sense, but that's part of the life of a Black man.

RECYCLED PRIORITIES

W hile throwing a 16 oz. empty glass bottle of apple juice into the garbage, a white person who saw my actions frowned and asked me if I didn't recycle glass and paper. In the most polite voice I could muster, which is pretty polite, I respond, "No" that I didn't and asked her how important it was to her. She replied it was very important. I could detect by the way she responded that she regarded my actions with abhorrence while considering her view or concern for the environment to be the epitome of how a model citizen should feel about recycling. I don't give a d### about recycling or saving animals. N#@$$ ARE DYING ON THE STREET LEFT AND RIGHT and the majority of White people, Hispanics, Asians and many Blacks don't give a d###. Why the $@##$^ would I be concerned about the d### environment when Black people are dying left and right and face some of the wildest conditions and obstacles. There is nothing worse than a N##r crying over some damn dead or dying whale when Black people are dying everywhere. People have just got to be kidding if they think I'm gonna spend time on issues such as concern for the environment and animals with all the other problems that are affecting us. That doesn't mean that the environmental pollution that is occurring in Black neighborhoods is not my concern, but when people talk about cleaning up the environment, they are not talking so much about addressing the toxic waste in Black neighborhoods, but instead are trying to save some d@$## endangered spotted owl in Washington.

FLASHING LIGHTS

A 55. 70. 75. 80. Motor spinning. Wheels turning. Head bobbing side to side. I was getting up and the car was getting down. The music was pumping. Bass was thumping. I was coolin'. Then it started. I ease off the gas and slowly love tap the brakes. I take a deep breath. I start to become jittery. I see a police car on the side of the highway ramp. I was at 55 when I passed him. He pulled out behind me. Ah-@#$. I gaze down at the speedometer. 55. 55. 55. That's what it said. My leg starts to jitter. I take another deep breath. D###, I was taking deep breaths ever since I saw the cop. I was trying to get myself together. Occasionally I would look in the rear view mirror. Not too often and not too sudden. The police car came closer. My heart beat started to pick up. This was it. I was going to be pulled over about something small, but it was going to quickly escalate into something big. The cop car pulled up on my left hand side. I concentrated on keeping my eyes fixed forward. I would see nothing but road. Please, I told myself, no sudden moves. Oh I hope I don't look like somebody who has recently committed a crime. Who am I kidding? They think we all look alike. Who am I trying to fool? Almost every police description is so ambiguous that it would cause for any of us to be picked up. The car I was driving was nice. It wasn't a Mercedes or a Beamer, but it was cool. An Acura. Not kited down, but still smooth. This is one of the few times I'm glad I don't have a Mercedes, Lexus or BMW, because then I definitely would have already been pulled over. I could feel the cop's eyes on me. Staring. I was waiting to hear the police sirens or to see the flashing light. Okay. Okay. Okay. Where is my driver's license. No I haven't had anything to drink. The registration is in the glove compartment. My license is in my wallet. I gaze back down at the speedometer. 55. The police car passes me by. D###, I wonder if White people feel like this. I wonder if White people become so tense when they see a police officer. Does their stomach curl like mine? Do they take a deep breath? Do they cut their eyes down in an attempt not to make eye contact. I don't know if don't know if they do, but almost every Brother I know does. It doesn't matter if they are lawyers or doctors. It doesn't mater whether they have a B.A. this or a J.D. that. I can only imagine how mentally racking it has to be for a young Black male teenager. My love, prayers and support goes out to all of them. I want them to understand that I understand their relationship to the man. The cop. It doesn't make a difference whether they are White or Black, because they almost all think blue. I am just trying to avoid ending up black and blue.

WATCH OUT A SNAKE WITH A KNIFE

I t is so wild, it just blows my mind. I just shrug my head and say, "D@$# this s!#$@ is wild." Politics are so corrupt and backstabbing...it just blows your mind. Almost every job or occupation will have will have some kind of inter-office politics going on, but in politics, it is unbelievable. If you think there are politics on your job, then imagine how much politics there is in politics. People will cut your throat without hesitation. People will cut your throat so fast and so smooth that until you actually take a step and your head falls off, you don't even know that it was cut. If you're going to be involved with politics, then you have to have a good needle and thread kit, because people put knives in your back all day. Not a day goes by in which someone doesn't try to do you some kind of harm. At the end of the day, you pull out your needle and thread kit and remove the daily knives that are stuck in your back in order that you can prepare for tomorrow. Some people have big

135

knives. Some people have small ones, but almost everybody you come into contact with has a knife. The only issue confronting you is under what circumstances would that person stab you in the back. Politics unfortunately is about making friends or associations with snakes. I remember a story that I was told several years ago that epitomized how you need to think when involved with politics. The story goes like this. It was a rainy, windy day. Think of thunderbolts and everything else that comes with a stormy, wet day. A man found a snake on the sidewalk that appeared to have been washed away by the storm. The snake looked injured and needed help. The man decided that he would take the snake home in order to make sure that it recovered. The snake recovered, and the man and the snake became best friends. The snake and the man would go everywhere together. The man fed the snake. Housed the snake. Spent quality time with the snake. It seemed like the perfect relationship. One day the man was sitting down watching television with the snake in its customary position around his neck. They were watching their favorite television show when all of a sudden the snake started to choke the man. In the beginning, the man thought it was a mistake and the snake was trying to position itself better around his neck. "Hey," the man thought to himself, "The snake and I are friends." The snake's grip around the man's neck became tighter. The man's eyes began to bulge and he told the snake, in a tone that implied that the snake was not cognizant of what it was doing, that it was choking him. The man assumed that once he informed the snake that it was choking him, that the snake would stop. A misunderstanding is what was occurring, the man thought. The snake began to tighten its grip, tighter and tighter and tighter. The man was now gasping for breath. He was panting as he frantically tried to pull the snake from his neck. Hot flashes and sweat streamed down the man's face. He pulled at the snake with all his strength. Finally, after numerous attempts, he was able to break the snake's grip from his neck and throw the snake across the room. Panting heavily and partially delirious, he asked the snake why did it choke him. The man started to tell the snake about all the things that they had done together. How the man had gone out of his way for the snake all the time, anytime and every time and how he felt the snake had done the same in many cases. How he had wished and wishes the snake the best in all that the snake has done and does. How he would never do anything to intentionally harm the snake. The man was totally puzzled by the snake's reaction. Finally, the snake told him what had never dawned on the man before. The snake said, "I was a snake when you met me, what did you expect?" The moral of this story is that in an environment full of snakes, never expect that you won't get bitten, no matter how good a working relationship or friendship you have or think you have established. If the opportunity presents itself and the award or awards are great, then don't be surprised to find a pair of fangs in your neck. Not all stabbings are with big butcher knives. Some of the most effective knifings occur through very small puncture holes which over time have the same effect as a large butcher knife, but in the early stages cannot be detected. It is important not to become overrun with anger or consumed with revenge. The Lord does not like ugly. You should invest time and energy to remove as many of the circumstances, flaws, or weaknesses, you can to limit the number of opportunities that you present to people to try to stab you in the back. You will always have some form of weakness, but the goal is to limit them as much as possible. People will always try to stab you in the back, so get used to that as a fact of life. I must tell you that even though I am cognizant of the political environment, my mouth still drops as I say to myself I can't believe what so and so just did. Above all, remember that no matter how friendly the situation appears, no matter how sweet a person seems, in the majority of cases there is more evil than good in most people with whom you will come in contact. Don't let your guard down, but at the same time don't let it be apparent that your guard is up. Keep your cool and always remember the rules of the game. If you can be got, there will always be a person or people trying to get you.

DON'T FORGET

There are certain events in your life that when they occur either confirm all that you have previously learned in life or send you searching for a whole new meaning of life and your role within it. One of my defining moments came as I sat in class, the sole African-American representative. The rest of the class was White except for a few other tokens. I was tearing the class up. The professor would ask a question, and I was ready to answer it right away. I made it a habit to always read several chapters ahead of whatever the professor assigned to the class, no matter how tired I was. I was on point. I answered so many questions that the professor purposely looked away from me in order to give other students a chance to answer. I would watch the professor's eyes as he reluctantly made eye contact with me so that I could answer another question. A White student sitting behind me nudged my chair. I felt my seat jerk. I leaned back in my seat and turned my head sideways to find out whether he was trying to get my attention or had accidentally bump my chair. He leaned forward and said, "Show off." I chuckled and said, "You're damn sure real." A few minutes later, I felt another tap on my desk. He slid his arm down low on the side of my desk and handed me a note. I opened the note and it confirmed what I had known all the time, but watched other Blacks who were joining me in my quest to be part of the higher socio-economic structure attempt to ignore. I now understand even better the conversations I had with my White peers in the hallways and at the local campus pub. The White people would always tell me how smart I was and how they were impressed with my analytical thinking. In the same sentence, they would express a level of sadness for me. It was as if they were telling me it was a shame for me to be so smart. There were also those who always found it in themselves to point out how I was a tribute to the Black race. They would say that I wasn't like the other Blacks and that more Blacks in my race needed to be more like me. There were other Whites who always looked at me as if they couldn't believe that a Black person knew something more than they did. The look on their faces was one of dismay. They looked at me like, "I'm gonna show you n@#$%." I always just chuckle. Back to the note. I opened it and read: "Do you feel as though you're a White man trapped in Black skin?" I buried my head in the cradle of my arms and placed the note on the desk, laughing hard internally. In a situation like this I could have several reactions. I could burst out in laughter like I did or I could cold beat down the White boy. I chuckled because I understood what he was trying to tell me. I was smarter than him. There was no question about it. No contest. His ability to lie about his ability to compete against me was overwhelmed by the direct evidence to the contrary. He could no longer live in that lie, so he created a solution to the lie. In order to maintain his definition of himself and his whiteness, he attributed my ability to outdo him in class to the possibility that I had some white in me. Actually, as far as he was concerned, I was a White man who had the unfortunate luck of being trapped in Black skin. To his logic, there was no way in his eyes that a Black person could be smarter than he was. I was a N@@#% and there was no way a N@#$% was smarter than him. If I were a White man whose life had accidentally and unfortunately been trapped in Black skin, that would make sense. He had equated intelligence with being White. The more intelligent I proved to be, the more white characteristics I possessed. I was way smarter than he, so there could only be one explanation, and that one explanation was that I was a White man trapped in Black skin. Of all the characteristics that are equated with being White, intelligence is the most important. Any Black person who possesses intelligence, therefore, must have some amount of White in him. This experience confirmed what I already knew but what some Black people spend a lifetime trying to hide from or ignore. A N@#$! is a N@#$! is a N@$@$. No matter how much we excel in anything, we will always be seen as N@#$@ in the White man's eyes. The issue is not our success in various academic fields or the extent to which we make stellar accomplishments. The issue is the definition of how many White people see themselves. If Black people as a whole are seen to possess some of the same intelligence characteristics that Whites possess, then White society would have to redefine their definition of themselves. In order that Whites don't have to redefine themselves, they instead render any accomplishment Black people make as extraordinary because it is unexpected. The issue of self-definition for many Whites is directly linked to how they see themselves and their role in the world. If White peoples' definition of themselves changed, so would their relation to the majority of the world of color have to change. It is more palatable for Whites to do as my college colleague did. Oh, by the way, my response to my peer was that I didn't feel that I was a White man trapped in Black skin but instead a Black man trapped in a White world. What I said went right over his head. That's another reason to chuckle... Professor, the answer to the question you asked is .....

SOLD

never selling cause I can't be sold; that's why I have never been bought. @$#!% it. I'm not selling out; I don't give a damn. This shit don't make no damn sense. Way too often I find myself shaking my head from side to side as I roll my eyes in the back of my head. I take a deep breath and just go "Woooo" and let out a chorus of "umph, umph, umph." As a Black person, you have enough problems in this world trying to deal with many White people, the last thing you want to have to deal with is fighting against your own people, but all too often that's the case. I'll tell you what. I'm not selling my soul. Too many Black people will sell their souls for a dollar. Sell their soul for a job. Just sell. Always selling. Always trying to get bought. It is hard as hell trying to maintain some form of Christian morals and values in this corrupt world. Every day is a struggle to maintain your sanity. So many people are trying to get over on you all the time. It just makes me sick.

I look deep into their fake smiles and I can see all the evil that's in them. It's some of my own people. That's what ticks me off. I can't understand how you sell out your own community. I can't understand how you stab people in the back for a dollar. A Job. Or for personal satisfaction. I don't understand how people get off abusing people, let alone your own people. But every day I see it. Every day, I don't understand it. Every day it keeps on happening. There are so many Black people doing harm against the Black community that they have to stand in line. Sad part about it is that these people often have the educational background or economic resources, or even both, to allow them to make a difference in bettering the lives of so many other Black people who are in despair. But nope, that's not where their head is. Instead, they spend their entire lives distancing themselves from the Black community and seeking to do harm against Black people whenever they can. The level of self-hate is unbelievable. You would think, with all the effort some Blacks give to distancing themselves from their community and making life difficult for other Blacks that somebody was giving awards somewhere. The s@#$ would be funny if it wasn't true. The saddest part about it is, people died. Literally died. I'm talking hung on trees. Set on fire. Eyes poked out. Whipped till their skin peeled off. Ostracized. Terrorized and if they stepped too far out of line to help themselves or other Black people: Homicide. People died in order to expand opportunities for Black people in a world that hates us because we are Black. How do some Blacks repay these blacks who made countless sacrifices? They hate Black people more than the people who taught them to hate themselves. It is so sad. I keep on going strong, and I want you to do the same thing. Love yourself. Love your community. Love God. In some distant world or place in the future, maybe we will be able to love each other without concern for race. For right now, I just want my own race to love itself. I want many of my Brothers and Sisters to remove the price tag from their bodies. The next time someone asks you what your price is, I want you to chuckle and look them dead in their face with your back straight and chest out and say, "Sorry, wrong person, I'm not for sale."

I KNOW YOU SAW ME

S low down. Ah-man you got to be kidding. Yo right here. Right here. Right here. This @$#@ is *!#@% up. Another cab zips past me. Why is it every time I try to hail a cab at night it automatically goes off-duty. Come on, now. I know everybody can't be going off-duty. Here I am an executive at a financial firm. I trade hundreds of millions of dollars of commodities every day and can't get a cab to take a $5.00 fare from me. It's late on a Saturday night. I have just come from visiting a co-worker at his crib. I decide to stroll over to another avenue to catch a cab. This is downtown. There are cabs everywhere, but not for a Brother. I have this problem sometimes, but never as much as I do tonight. Then it dawns on me. I look down at myself. A Nike warm-up with matching sneakers and a baseball cap. There was no Wall St. Journal. There was no Georgio-Armani double breasted suit with a matching leather attache case. No spit-shined polished leather shoes.

No Rolex watch. I was dressed casually for a light evening of fun and laughter. My partner and I had seen a movie and had gone back to his house to cool out. Now how the hell was I going to get across town? We lived about 27 blocks apart. I was tired and in no mood to catch a train or walk. The clouds opened up and gave me an evening treat. Exactly what I don't need. "Yo-Yo-Yo-Yo. Right here. Right here. You bastard." The cab bypasses me and goes half a block up to pick up a White man in clothes that are definitely raggedy in contrast to my well coordinated sweat suit. The cloud treat is starting to be a little too much to bear standing still. I begin to stroll, occasionally backwards, as I look for a cab. There was no cab coming for me. There was no need to fool myself. I was a N@#$!. I dropped my head down low between my shoulders and began a light jogging pace. I could imagine how hard it was for the average Brother to catch a cab. Here I am thinking I'm above average. Well one thing is for sure, when the cab driver sees me, I'm no special N@#!$. I pick up the pace a little. The rain is coming down a little too hard to be running cute. I run into a grocery store in order to avoid the rain. D###, stop staring at me. I'm not going to rob the store. I'm just trying to get out of the rain for a hot second. Look, I'm gonna buy something. D@#$, you're still staring at me. Well I'm gonna browse around the store for a few minutes until the rain slows down. You will just have to stare at me. Eventually the rain slowed down, and I proceeded to jog on my way home. I stopped looking for a cab that night. I didn't even want to give anybody my hard earned money. I was just going to do a little running and walking until I got home. What the hell, if slaves could walk from the South to the North to flee slavery, I d@#$ sure could walk a couple of blocks. A cab stops at the red light. The cab driver and I make eye contact. He quickly turns his head around and slams on the accelerator as the light turns green. I love you, too.

I DON'T WANT IT

The fear of AIDS just has not hit me. I'm extremely conscious of its ramifications, but it still doesn't seem to click. I look back at the number of people with whom I have slept, and I just say "D@#$." It's nervously funny, but even though I know all that I know about AIDS, there are only a few women I regret having slept with. In my life, as though I could be talking about somebody else's life, I have slept with over 50 women. For many that may seem a lot, others may say I'm not even in their league. But when I say I have slept with over 50 women, I'm not lying on my @#$%!. I'm just telling it like it is. Sometime I catch a flu and panic, because I don't know whether it could be signaling the beginning of a much bigger disease. Namely AIDS. I'm extremely scared to take the HIV test, because I'd rather not know whether I have something. If you knew that you had AIDS, then your whole life would change. I would rather just die. Let me add to this that I'm really in good health, at least I hope and pray I am. I remember when the word came out that Magic Johnson was HIV-POSITIVE. Every Brother I knew or spoke to said, "Not my N@#$!." It wasn't that we were oblivious to the fact that Magic probably was hitting @#$ left and right, but that he was our N@#$#. If my man could get it, then d@#$% (Whooh). That was some @#$%. Every Brother I knew basically said that was @#$%! up, but I don't remember anybody saying they were going to stop hitting @#$ or that we were going to exist in a monogamous relationship. The best I can remember is that Brothers said they were going to try to be more selective in the Sisters they might hit. I never understand what Brothers mean by that, but I say it too. It is as though Brothers who have problems adding up basic arithmetic all of sudden can calculate the statistical probability of a particular Sister giving them AIDS. How the hell we compute the average, I don't know, but I have done it myself. I think it did make us more conscious of the need to use condoms for protection, but even that is not a guarantee. If sperm can get past a condom, then so does AIDS, but if you can reduce the being exposed to something, then do it. I guess do it. Don't try to deceive yourself that by using a condom only, that you are automatically protected from AIDS. I don't want to get off the point which is I don't know what it will take for the African-American community to understand the significance of AIDS. Especially since AIDS is spreading disproportionately in the African-American heterosexual community. It's not an information issue, even though the more information available the better. I think AIDS will only become important when we decide to make it important. Unfortunately that is not now.

EVIDENCE ALWAYS FOUND
BUT NEVER LOST

Get outta here...I know you playing...Word...Tell me it ain't so...Damn...It's a doggone shame what a Sister will do," I told my partner as he explained that he had found a pair of this girl's underwear in his dresser draw. "Check the bathroom did she leave a toothbrush?" I asked. "Hold on one second," he replied as he left the phone. Before he even came back to the telephone, I could hear him saying, "I can't believe this s#%!@." I started to chuckle and laugh as I asked him, "What happened?" "She left a f#@# toothbrush," he said as if he was mad as hell. I started to crack up, screaming into the phone with laughter. "That s##% ain't funny," he said in a tone of voice which meant for me to stop laughing even though it was funny. "Yes that $#!% is. Don't lie. You know its funny," I responded as my laugh shifted to a chuckle with a smirk on my face. "Ouch, what the h@#$ is this?" he yelled back through the phone. "This s#@$ don't make no f#$#!% sense," he said to himself or to me. "What's wrong, Man?" I asked "What's wrong, Man?", I repeated. "I found an earring." I could tell he was really fed up. She was out and she didn't even know it. She had thought she was claiming her turf by leaving little things around my main man's apartment. The earring, the toothbrush, the underwear were all collectively supposed to serve notice, a form of Sister voodoo used to scare off other Sisters by making a statement in her absence that she existed, or at least somebody existed and would be coming back. "Get the f#%! outta here," I said as I shook my head from side to side and murmured, "Umph, umph, umph.". I wasn't shocked, I had been through it too. Everybody who has his own place or has lived in a college dorm room has experienced the same thing. It usually starts off innocently. A Sister who you have been giving the pipe to arrives at your place for an overnight stay. I'm talking about a preplanned overnight stay. Not a I hit the a## and she ended up staying over, but what I said: A preplanned overnight. You have been tapping

160

the a## off and on and eventually she stays over for a weekend or a couple of days. Two nights. Maybe three, but never four. You go to pick her up, and she has about twenty million suitcases. You look at all the suitcases and the big overnight type bag she has and you wonder where the #%!# is she going. You just stare at the luggage and say to yourself, what the #!%$ did she think I said. I know, or should I say, I hope for her that she didn't confuse what I said to mean that she is moving in. I said "week-end". You try to figure how she could confuse weekend with what looks like several months of clothes. You smile at her and say, "You got whole lot of stuff." She replies that "it's not a lot" and that she needs everything that she has. You grin back and say okay, but you don't understand that #$%# at all. You don't want to say anything that will cause for her not to come over, but at the same time you're not thrilled about her bring all that shit over to your apartment. "Are you ready?" you ask her as you begin to carry some of the multiple bags. You survive carrying them to the car and bringing them into the apartment. You know how you survive. You survive because you psyche yourself up that you're going to make sure that when she leaves every little piece of s### that she brought with her goes right out the f##$%# door with her when she leaves. I'm talking about everything. When its time for her to leave, you start looking around the apartment to see whether or not you see anything that belongs to her. You check the closet to make sure that all the clothes she took all that time to hang up went right back in that suitcase. You check under the bed for a bra, blouse, underwear, t-shirt. You name it. You check for it. You look over your dresser to see if there is any fingernail polish or anything else that could have accidentally gotten "mixed up" with yours. You check every place in the apartment before she leaves. You take all her stuff and pack it back in the car, and before you get ready to pull away you say, "Hold on one second." She says, "What's wrong?" "I will be right back," you respond as you go back in the apartment to make one more quick glance. Then you're off. "Money, why she leave all this s### in my apartment?" my partner asked. We both knew the answer, but I pretended for a second that I didn't. "You know damn well," I replied. "That's the quickest way to get cut," my partner responded in a way to indicate that she was fired from her position of being sexed. No SEX is worth that hassle. Well, I shouldn't say no sex, just not this sex. To this day, Sisters still leave stuff all around the apartment. I put everything in a box. I have Sandra's earrings. Cheryl's bra. Krystal's jeans. Nancy's blouse. Kim's nail polish. This girl Carol even left a shoe. By the way, any Sisters needing a Nine West blue pump size 8 1/2 for your left foot, please call 478-0976.

GOOD MORNING

know your game. I see you. Don't front. I got your cards. You won't sell me a dream. I know what time it is. You think you're slick. You think you're cute. You think you can pull something over my eyes. I'm not a new jack. There is no rookie who lives here. I know the real deal. You won't play me for a sucker. I see your eyes on my pockets. Trying to figure a way to get in them. You think by giving up the a## you're going to get paid. Nope, I'm not the one. I'm hip to your game. I can't count the amount of times I found myself murmuring those words to myself regarding a Sister. I saw you, but you didn't smile. I looked you dead in your eyes as you tried to avoid making eye contact. I was only going to say, "Good morning." I had no agenda, I was just trying to be friendly. You didn't want that. You did everything to avoid being friendly. You assumed that just because I might say "hello" that I wanted something. No, I don't want your number. No, I don't want to know where you live. No, I don't care if we can get together sometime. I don't have to pull up on you, we will meet again. I know you. I know your game even though we have never met before. You did me wrong before. I remember it well. I spoke to you in the elevator. It was a nice day. The sun was shining bright, and the sky was crystal clear. I said, "It sure is a nice day outside." I waited for your response. There was no response. "It really looks nice I outside," I repeated in another way, as if I was saying it for the first time. You gave me some soul-sister up and down head nod. There were no words. No eye contact. Nothing but a nod. I chuckled to myself inside. D@##, shortie to trying play me to left. I was respectful. I had made a pleasant statement. Nothing was derogatory, but you played me local. A White man got on the elevator. We were dressed the same way. Navy blue suit and tie. Wing tipped shoes. Starch white shirt. Conservative looking tie with a Wall Street Journal. I had the look of somebody who had assimilated into the Eurocentric mainstream, but I was only playing the game. I would never give up my soul or let somebody take my soul. I compared what me and the White boy had on and concluded we may have caught some of the same sales. He turned and smiled at you. I watched your face light up. I saw the dimples appear. I saw the eyes glitter. I just stared. He then said "Good Morning." Quickly you shot back "The temperature is 78 degrees, the wind-chill factor is x over y and this is due to the cloud and star alignment, and tomorrow's temperature will be this and that." Maybe I'm exaggerating the temperature stuff but not the smile. The smile you gave him but refuse to give to me. I never forget it. Not that I can cause you do it to me every day. You always look past me. Around me. Trying your best not to make eye contact with someone of your own race. I chuckle to myself, cause I know we will meet again. You will hear about me or of me and then it begins. I'm the same person, but you're not. Now you know I'm paid. You know I got it going on, and you're trying to get on. That is get on mine. You quickly try to make up for trying to play me for a sucker in the beginning. I'm hip to your game, though. I told you before, I know the real deal. Now you want to huddle with me. You want to cuddle me. Mouth all open now. I can see nothing but teeth. Grinning and smiling in front of me ear to ear. Now you want to be with me. I laugh to myself internally and at you at the same time. Don't worry, you're going to get paid. You're going to get paid no mind. I'm going to sex you and step. You had no use or role for me before. Now you want to be with me. I have no respect for you now. I'm just going to do you and move on. Revenge is in effect. If I don't get you, my man is going to get you, because we know the deal. Don't give me that, it's hard to find a Brother, stuff. There are some of us out here, but you bypass us with your attitude. You can't even find those of us who are eligible, hard-working and together Brothers because of the way you look for us. You come at us with game and then get mad when you get gamed. You try to sell me a dream and end up getting sold. That's it. That's enough. You get the true deal. Maybe next time you will smile. I'm smiling at you now.

KNOCK, KNOCK WHO IS IT? VANILLA

This is the deal. The truth must be told. It's a question that goes through many Brothers' heads. They want to know how it feels to hit a White girl. The issue is whether or not there is a difference between chocolate and vanilla. Well, all I can do is give you my experience. Just before you get ready to make penetration, you say to yourself--this is it -- as a chuckle cuts across your face. I finally am going to know whether or not there is a difference between Black and White b### and whether or not one of them is more juicer or more sweeter. Let me take you back to how the scene first unfolded. It was about two o'clock in the morning, I had just finished watching CNN sports so I was about to knock out. I dove onto the bed, buried my face into the pillow without pulling back the bedspread and began to crash. All of a sudden I heard a knock at the door. The knock was rather soft and delicate. I listened to the knock for a few seconds before responding.

When I heard the knock, I squinted up my face and placed my ear in the direction of the door as if that somehow would identify the knocker. I decided I would creep to the door and ask, "Who is II?" with the deepest baritone voice I could muster. The voice said "ils Nancy." I paused for a second said "Humph" as I tried to figure why she was knocking on my door at this time, while simultaneously opening it up. "What's up?" I asked friendly but with a serious undertone. "I wondered if you were studying, because I have a major exam tomorrow, and I'm having trouble staying up by myself?" she said with a forced grin that said, please let me in, come on. "Cool, come on in," I replied with a bit of suspicion, which is always healthy. I told her she could use the desk in the corner of the dorm room to study because my roommate no longer lived here, as though as a Black person in the dorm they didn't already know my comings and goings and who lived or visited. She sashayed over to the desk as I checked out the baby doll lingerie outfit she had on. I checked out the lace on the outfit and how the bottom of the fabric barely covered that white a##. I immediately shut the thought out of my mind, because lots of n#### have died for looking, let alone hitting, white a##, and I'm not trying to get lynched. Whether you get lynched on a tree or lynched in a court, you are still one dead N####. I proceeded to go over to my books which were stacked evenly with my pen and pad on the side and began to fake doing work. I had already studied for the last several hours. I really just wanted to tell her "no" I wasn't studying, but who knows whether there would be a time when I would need something from her or something else could come up and she could help me, but wouldn't, because I had turned her down. What the h##, I would do more studying. There was a time when slaves weren't allowed to read, so it won't hurt reading a little bit more before crashing out. Matter of fact, it will help me. I opened up my Chemistry book to chapter 3 and began to read. After a couple of pages, I found myself reading a page then flipping over to the next page without completely reading the last one. My head started to jerk back as I caught myself dosing off. I began to read the second paragraph on page 78 with intensity until it dawned on me that I was already up to page 81. I couldn't even remember reading page 78. This is the best indicator that it is time to knock out. I decided to let her know that I was gonna get ready to knock out, cause I'm more beat than I thought. I also planned to wish her the best with her studying and her exam, as I placed that familiar fake grin on my face that White people always give to Blacks. It's that grin when they are smiling at you when they shake your hand and keep on smiling at you, and you're like, what the f### are you smiling at me for. You smile back raising the top of your eyebrows with a grin that says, I don't understand why we're doing this but I'll go along with it anyway. Not to lose track, so I turned around and began to tell her it was time for me to call it a night. Hold up one d@## second. I looked and then I squinted my eyes to look even closer, then a devilish grin cuts across my face as my head rocks back, "Whooo." I started to chuckle and say to myself, be cool, be cool. I had just noticed that Nancy hadn't brought any books to study, but instead was sitting in the corner with her baby doll outfit on in the dark. I gained my composure and ask her if she was alright? She said yes and nodded her head once. On the second nod she lowered her gaze and leveled it at my crotch and blew a soft kiss. I sighed "oh-boy" and then said something about I needed to call my main man. I dialed the digits on the phone unaware of what I was going to say to my man but knew we had to rap. As I heard the phone ringing, I begin to see an image of myself on the cover of Jet magazine saying that I didn't do it. An article next to my photo alleges that I have date-raped a White girl. You know the real deal though. The White girl's parents, friends or somebody on that level find out or are told that she is sleeping with a Black man and then they confront her. She's scared of the family reaction to her sleeping with a Black man, so she comes up with the story that a Black man date raped her. The next thing you know a brother is sitting in a cell. The phone was still ringing. I thought of how sisters would respond if they knew I was about to sex a White girl especially with all the eligible Black Sisters there were out here. There were no excuses and in many ways they are right. If Sisters found out I was about to sex a White girl I would be blackballed or I would have to have enough money so that it didn't matter to some of the cheesy Sisters, as long as I slept with them next. D### my man won't pick up the phone. I turned back around and put on the smile. I put on one of those cheesy smiles that you know are fake. She came over to me and asked me if I like her at all. I didn't respond but instead just smiled back. She then asked me if she should leave. I said, "Stay for a while." There it is. I have just sealed my fate. I'm gonna hit the White a##. She lays back on the bed and I begin to kiss her on her neck. This was not going to be any love-making thing. This was pure sex. Unquestionable Sin. I knew better though. I knew, I should choose the Word of God versus the world. The Savior versus Sin. Unfortunately, I was weak and didn't depend on the Lord to make me whole. My actions were truly saying who I loved. I was more than just a sinner but a hyprocite. I talked love but I loved lust. Therefore, I was going to tear this a## up like I had never torn a## up before. When I split those legs I went into her so strong and so deep I wanted to hear screams so loud that she would make the face for screaming but no words would come out. For every brother who ever died for looking at White a## or for sleeping with it I was going to make up for them. I was going to tear this b## up. If it was the Black d### she wanted, then she was going to get more of it then she could ever imagine. I had just dedicated my life to living up to ever Mandingo fantasy she every had about Black d###. She was going to go back and tell her White friends about this experience and have all of them drooling about how it was to sleep with a Black man. After all the screams and all the multiple orgasms she had, I told her to break out. She left shivering wondering when we would do this again. I had already made up in my mind it would never happen again, but I just didn't tell her on the spot. She tiptoed out of the room as she looked back and giggled. I closed the door and sat at my desk with my feet on top of the desk and just sighed. I felt like a traitor to the Sisters. More importantly I should have felt like a traitor to God. This was more than just about race but also about my desire to race to sin. I knew better. I also knew that White a## was not better than chocolate no matter how much some people said that white a## was better or that it was all the same. Chocolate is what I like. I now knew she had gotten more out of the deal than me. Every time I see that white girl, she still shivers when she looks at me. I chuckle because the only chocolate she will ever get from me again is Ben & Jerry's. My chocolate and my emotions will be for one person and that one person will be someone who is the same flavor.

DID YOU HEAR THAT?

She's a hoe. Slut. Sleep with me. I slept with her. Sex me baby. All I wanna do..Take it off. Tear it off. I'm gonna get off. Hard on. I'm on her. She's on mine. I knocked it, tapped it, slapped it, flipped it, hit it. I macked it. Station to station, I listened. You could not but be consumed by it. Sex on top of sex on top of sex. Slowly I stopped shaking my head from side to side to the beat. My eyebrows cut down. My forehead wrinkled. I decided to just sit down and listen to words of the songs more carefully. I rested my chin the palm of my hand as I leaned forward with elbows near my knees.. D###, I thought, almost ever word or every phrase was about sexing somebody. A body. A person. A real person. A Sister. An aunt. A cousin. A niece. A future Black mother. Somebody's daughter. There was no love. No emotions. No feelings. There was nothing, but sex, sex and more sex. Oh-man, I thought to myself, what is going on. What are we as Black people saying to each other, about each other and wishing to do to each other? Teenage pregnancy, rape, physically abusive relationships, running trains and other forms of debasing images of Black women have existed way before certain contemporary forms of music. There is growing tendency by many in the Black community to attempt to attribute the social ills that afflict the African-American community to solely that of hip-hop. They are obsessed with blaming hip-hop for all the social ills that afflict today's youth. There is obviously a correlation between the two in regards to certain youth internalizing the messages conveyed in different songs. However it must be quickly pointed out that these social ills existed prior to that of hip-hop. A more compelling question that is not asked often enough is, what is it about these derogatory and debasing images of ourselves that is depicted in these songs that is causing us or many of our youth to gravity to them? I can't count the number of times I have worked or attended a concert in which the entertainer was shouting/singing or rapping to the women in the audience that they were hoes, b####, sex toys or sluts. The entertainer would say how he wanted to "c### in so and so mouth" and how he was going to "sex you today and your friend tomorrow." The entertainer would go on about how all he wanted to do was sex you today and leave, not tomorrow, but leave you that same day. I would look around and I would see women jumping up and down smiling and saying "Take me, Take me, Take me. Sex me, Sex me, Sex me." I would hear them say "He's so cute. I wanna get with him." I would look and shrug my head. Here this Brother is singing or rapping this song about how much lack of respect he has, not only for you, but for Sisters who look like you while your jumping up and down to the beat and screaming, "I love you." Don't give me no d### story about you just listen just to the beat. You hear the words too,. Don't play me slow. I know what time it is. Just say you don't give a d@## but don't try to front like you don't hear the lyrics or how it potrays you negatively. I listen to some of the most popular music today and shake my head. Many of the experiences recanted in the songs unfortunately I have done. This makes the song, real but not right. Many of the things I had done were wrong. Not everything, but many of the things. Some of the things I did wrong I knew and some I found out as I became wiser. Many of the lyrics I hear not only describe what are often true events, but glorify them as the way things should be. At times I could be jumping up and down and shaking my head to a song, and then I become real sad. I feel real sad for the Sisters who are constantly bombarded by negative images of themselves. I feel sorry for the Sisters who internalize the messages conveyed in songs as being the way they need to live or the way they should act. I feel sorry for the Black community. How are we as people going to progressively address the various political, social, and economic issues confronting us here in the United States and abroad if we are sending and glorifying negative images and portrayals of ourselves? If another community portrayals us in a negative way, then that's one thing, but when we do it to ourselves, that is another. It seems strange to me, but I find it rather odd, or should I say difficult, to envision the Black community addressing successfully various issues that affect our well-being when at home there exists so much friction between Black men and Black women. I know we have been steadily moving forward, or sometimes barely slipping back, but if we are to make strong strides forward as a people, we will have to reexamine again and again how we as Black men and women relate to each other. I don't think the answer is censorship of music. I think the answer has to be internal to us. As long as it is profitable to make records depicting us in a certain way or doing certain things, there will always be record companies, and unfortunately certain Brothers and Sisters, who are more than willing to partake in this type of detrimental harm to our community. The images of ourselves will only change when we no longer tolerate, individually or collectively, our being depicted a certain way. When the majority of Blacks make it unprofitable to see us in certain ways then we will start to see a drastic decline in certain imageries of ourselves. Until that time, we will continue to look, sound and dance in a way that depicts us in a derogatory and debasing way.

WHY WE SLEEP WITH SO MANY WOMEN?

Here I am sitting on the couch with my right hand in my drawers, cupping my b### as I flick the remote control on the T.V. set from channel to channel. Sweaty drawers and shorts, a glass of O.J. and an air conditioner on high. "Oh-Boy." I utter to myself to indicate that I am tired. I had just dropped 25 points in this summer basketball tournament and was bushed. I sat around for a few minutes trying to see if there was anything on cable I wanted to watch before I prepared to take a shower. I couldn't shake from my mind the conversation the Brothers and I had regarding why we sleep with so many Sisters. It was one of those conversations we never really have, so when we had it, everybody put in their two cents. After a big game like today, the fellas sit around on the park bench and look at all the a## that was walking through the park, standing near the sidelines or sitting in a beach chair watching the basketball games. About right now I would be giving a pound to the different people on my opponent's squad and telling them good game. I would then see a Brother I knew from way back in the day. We would make eye contact and I would hear him shout, "Oh s##%, my N@@%#." We would walk up to each other and give each other a soul pound as we patted each other's back and embraced. The next thing you know we would be reminiscing about the past and bursting out in laughter. I would make a motion toward the park bench, and the Brother and I would proceed to join the other fellas. As I walk, I place my thumbs in my waistband and push my shorts down. I would lift up the bottom of the inside of my t-shirt and wipe the sweat off the brow of my forehead. Brothers would be talking about who got slammed on. Who got shook crazy hard. Who got pinned on the boards or ripped. How so and so needs to give the ball up quicker when he is in the lane or why so and so knows d### well they shouldn't be taking certain shots and how they need to cut that s### out. A Brother would say something about how if money had thrown one more elbow, he didn't give a f### how much of a non-violent tournament this was suppose to be, he was gonna break that ##%@##$ up on the spot. Today had been a good day. We had won the game and were advancing in the tournament, and there was crazy sex everywhere. My main man pointed out this Sister he was trying to bone as another Brother tapped me on the shoulder and asked me if I knew who was hitting the girl with the cut off shorts. I told him everybody had hit that a##. I looked around and you could see a bunch of Brothers nodding in agreement. Then it began. A Brother started to tease one guy about all the ugly looking Sisters he had boned. The Brother responded back that not only were the sisters he had sexed not ugly but that the Brother had nerve. He then told the Brother that anybody like him who was always lying on their d### should be happy to get anybody, because right now his a## is not getting no a##, let alone good a## or lots of good a##. All of sudden Brothers screamed in laughter. Brothers were falling off the benches onto the ground. My main man was on his back with his legs up in the air crying in laughter. I was on the concrete on my knees, slapping the palm of my hand against the ground and hollering. We were having a great time. Brothers love to talk about sports and sex. I don't care if you are a doctor, lawyer, hustler or pimp. College educated, high school graduate/attending or drop out. It doesn't matter. We all talk about, or once talked about, a## we had, a## we're getting and a## we're trying to get. The topic of sex and sports was one in which Brothers could always find unity and share experiences. Then he said it. I still don't understand why. Mouths were opened, brothers were staring into space or the ground as we contemplated the question of why we sleep with so many Sisters. One Brother said, "What's wrong with you, N####r?" and another asked, "What he say?" but the reality of it was that we had all heard what he had said and were all frozen by it. Everybody kind of looked at each other to see if somebody was going to say something or if the subject could be ignored by chuckling it away. There would be no ignorance.

The subject floodgates were open. I can still hear Ant, which is short for Anthony, saying, "The majority of Sisters be hoeing.I don't trust nobody, so I'm f#### everybody. Everybody who wants to give me the a## who looks good, I'm f##%@#. Thats my comment. I'll tell you why, too. I remember when I was regular. I had no loot and was struggling. My clothes were well kept, but they weren't always name brand or crazy hip. I was a nice guy and basically am one today. Sisters paid me no mind. Do you hear me? No mind. They gave me no dap. Everywhere I turned I heard the word, "NO". Some sisters would roll their eyes in their head and would look at me and say "please". They made me feel crazy low. Now look at me. I have crazy loot. Mad dough. Sisters are now on my d###. They ain't nothing but money hungry b####. Ever since I cut the record deal and went on tour, everything has been different. The same b#### who had no time for me are now all on my d###. Sweating me day and night. I don't trust no hoe. So yes, I'm a dog. Bow-wow, bow-wow. Woof, woof." I can still see Ant swinging his hips back and forth as he simulated sexing a Sister and barking out, "Woof, woof. Woof. Woof, woof. Woof." My man Irv had this crazy serious look on his face. You could tell that he was really into the conversation and wanted to say something, but that he first wanted Ant to finish everything he had to say. When Irv finally spoke, I didn't know what he was going to say, but I knew he was sincere. "You know," Irv began, "I don't even know why. I never asked myself before. This s### is wild, but I can't even tell you. I just do it. I have never really sat down like we are doing now and thought about it. The first thing that comes to my head is because you're supposed to. To a Sister, that s### may sound crazy weird, but it makes perfect sense to me. Its part of being a man. The more women you sleep with, the more respect you get from your partners. It's a popularity thing. People give you respect or a certain amount of dap if you can get Sisters, especially good-looking Sisters to sleep with you. It's just another way to fit in, I guess. F### it. I give up with this guessing s##%. I'm just happy I'm getting a##." "I'll tell you what," cut in my man 'D'. "I get tired of Sisters trying to use sex as a bargaining tool. Sisters always say s###t like this to their girlfriends: 'If Tone doesn't act right, then he won't get none, or if he don't take you out girlfriend, then don't give him none." They say other dumb sh### like 'He better act right or he will never get none, or, 'he won't get this again acting the way he does.' It is always about if you don't do this they you don't get none. If you don't buy me this, take me out here then you won't get none. Almost everything Sisters do is about making a Brother feel that if he doesn't do certain things, then he won't get the a##. It's all about power and control. Once you get the a##, you find out it isn't all that and you move to the next one and the next one and the next one. Once a Sister comes at me like that, then I'm just trying to get the drawers and step. You know, step with the quickness." When my man Steve, alias "Slick Daddy," got up, I knew we were all in for it. I braced myself and just waited patiently. Then he began. "Y'all mother-#### are bugging. Trying to make this s### complicated. Let me simplify this ##%# for you. P##%# is good. That s#@## feel good. When that warmth goes around your d###, that #@%# be good. I'm not making no excuses for what is a human function. Sex is normal. I like it. It's good, and I'm trying to get as much of it as possible. Mother##%@# who say all p#%## is the same is lying. That s#@## is different. Some s#@## is deep and some s@#@# is tight. Some Sisters know how to shake that a## and others don't. It's not always about getting a nut, but it is also about the hunt. The chase to get a nut is what makes certain nuts special. That's all I'm gonna say about this s###." "Oh s##%t, did you see that slam. Money peed all over him." It was over. Just a quick as the conversation began, it was over. The slam dunk this kid did on this Brother was so nasty that it had diverted everyone's attention. The moment was gone. We never got a chance to get crazy deep. It seemed as if we had only scratched the surface. I look back at the conversation and all the postulating Brothers did, and I know something was missing. No one made reference to whatever insecurities they had as a man. No one mentioned how the sexist society we live in devalues women and therefore our actions reflect that attitude. I didn't hear anyone talk about the role slavery may play in Black men's psyche. No mention of how sex provides a vehicle of empowerment for Black men in a world in which they feel subjugated. Most importantly, I didn't hear any reference to God and how we had strayed away from the Lord's Commandments. There was a lot we didn't hadn't said, but at the same time, there was a lot we had. This wasn't a convention or conference, but instead Brothers cooling out and vibing together. I believe there was some truth in everything that the brothers said, but I still feel like there is something missing. A piece of the puzzle that I, nor they have, ever explored. You would think with AIDS and everything else, we would talk about this more often. Maybe, and I do mean maybe, after today's conversation we will.

DANCING TO THE WRONG BEAT

Dancing. Dancing. Dancing. Never reading. Never picking up a book. Party over here. Party over there. No newspaper. No magazines. No journals. Gettin' over. Gettin' down. Gettin' my groove on. Federal and state legislation is passed by various legislative bodies impacting the quality of life of millions of African-Americans. Page me. Call me on the cell. Meet me at the club. Every day various economic partnerships and alliances are forged throughout the world having immense impact on the economic condition of people of African descent throughout the Diaspora. Where the party at? Don't scratch my CD. Educational summits and hearings are being conducted to determine the educational curriculum that will be taught to our children. What's the name of that new song? Did you see that video last night? Black colleges, which have provided high quality and accessible education for hundreds of thousands, are under constant attack. I'm

193

telling you the beat on the track is slamming. Newly constructed congressional districts which were developed to address the lack of minority representation in federal and state legislative bodies have been threatened by the conservative right wing's reinterpretation usage of the Civil Rights Act. The very laws we fought to create are now often being used by our adversaries to stifle our progress. I gotta get that tape. The music be pumping. As we enter into a more scientific and technologically advanced society in the 21st century, the masses of Blacks in our community lack the necessary computer skills to compete in the ever-changing global economy. Now how much are those sneakers? A disproportionate number of African-Americans are inflicted with AIDS. What time does this club close? Black male incarceration rates exceed Black male college enrollment. Party. I got to go to party. Where's the party. Who's having a party. What time is the party. Let's party. There is just to d### much P-A-R-T-Y-I-N-G going on.

IT JUST AIN'T RIGHT

Where did you go, and why aren't you here?" I catch myself mumbling to myself. That s### ain't right. I don't know what went down between you and my mother, but I'm here. I'm here. How the hell can you ignore the fact that I'm alive? Okay, I can understand that you f###% up your life and that it's hard to get a job and you can't contribute any money. I didn't ask you for any money, even though some money d##% sure would be good. You could show up every once in a while and check up on how I'm doing. If you f##%# up your life, you could at least tell me things to avoid me bogging down my own. You could tell me about your mistakes so that maybe I don't make them. If you think your mistakes are your business or you feel embarrassed to tell me or anything like that, then you just say, "Look, I f##%# up my life, but don't f##%# yours." You could say that you're proud of what I'm trying to do with my life. You could tell me to keep on going strong. You could tell me that there is nothing out on the streets and that you are living proof. You don't even have to degrade yourself. You could just find things to uplift me. These things will never make up for the fact that you are not around, but they would allow me to know you give a d##%#. I ask myself "How could a Black man desert his blood?" Then I look around, and I see so many other Brothers without fathers, just like me. It's not right. It's not that Moms doesn't try her best, but there are things that affect me as a Black man that you understand. You might not give me the right answer on what to do, but you could at least validate that I'm not crazy. Some days I think about you, but most of the time I just try to block you out. When I do think about you I just shake my head and say, "That s### ain't right. It just ain't right. Pops, that s##% ain't right, wherever you are."

SOMEDAY NOT JUST THE BASKETBALL COURT

Clap. Clap. Yo-oo. I catch the ball in the middle of the air and do a stutter step cross over dribble as I throw the ball behind my back to the man cutting on my right-hand side. My teammate catches the ball and jumps up in the air as if he is going to shoot a jumper. Instead he passes the ball to another Brother who is cutting down the baseline. The Brother on the baseline catches the ball and makes a no-look pass to me sprinting down the middle of the lane. I catch the ball and elevate crazy high. Everybody assumes I'm gonna dunk the ball, but instead I make a sweet finger roll. The ball glides off my finger tips into an upward spiral. The ball elevates and elevates until finally it comes down straight through the net. "D### that was pretty," I hear people saying. "Ah-shokie, Brothers trying to do something now," I overhear a bystander saying.

"It's going to get heated out here, Shortie", says a Brother to another Brother on the side lines as he gives his man a pound. I land on the ground after laying the ball up and start to shuffle backwards. I drift back to the other end of the court in order to play D. The expression on my face says, "You haven't seen nothing yet." As a Brother comes across the half court line, he tries to split two defenders knowing d##% well that his skill level does not allow that option. You hear people in the crowd say "rip" as my teammate steals the ball. One of the guy's teammates who the ball was stolen from shrugs his head and says, "Give up the rock, man." My teammate who stripped him of the ball is dribbling down court incredibly fast. There is only one defender on the opposing team who is back to play defense. My teammate then tosses the ball up toward the rim. Unknown to the opposing player, another player on my team has cut the baseline and has started to elevate. By the time the opposing teammate notices my teammate, he has already got his knees in the guys chest and his hands way above the rim. My teammate catches the ball at rim level and cocks his arm backwards before slamming the ball down through the rim. The people on the sidelines are going crazy. My teammate lets out a gigantic yell as he hangs on the rim. The opposing player has this s@## face expression that says d@#@. I scream out "Yeah Money." The Brothers on my team come back down the court to play defense. All of the guys on our team give them either a high five, a pound or a smack on the a#@. A brother on my team says "That's what I'm talking about." We all start to buckle down and play defense. The most interesting thing about the interaction that took place on the basketball court is that nobody on my team knows each other. We were five strangers whose lives had been thrust together on a basketball court. We had never met before. We didn't know any relatives of each other or anything. We didn't go to school together and some maybe didn't even attend school. The only thing we have in common that is apparent is that we love basketball and have the athletic skill to play the game on a competitive level. With all the teamwork and coordination that we display, it may seem to some people that we know each other. If you look at the way we encourage each other and give each other high-fives when we score, you would think we had been friends for a long time. By the way we scold each other, you would think that there is a friendship that has existed over time that allows us to do that. At times, we argue with the other team about whose ball it is after a controversial play. We would argue about whether so and so had stepped out of bounds, if he had traveled, if so and so had been fouled, the list could go on forever. Every once in a while, heated words are exchanged. A fight would almost begin. Brothers on the court would be like, break that s###% up and play ball. Brothers would murmur some words under their breaths and then go back to playing the game. After the game was over, Brothers would walk passed the opposing team players and give them a pound and say, "Good game." Brothers would start taking practice shots at the hoop until whoever has next selected his team and the winning team had caught its breath. Every time a Brother hit a jumper from a respectful distance then, whoever caught the ball falling out of the net would then pass it back to him. The guy would keep on shooting until he missed, and then whoever got the rebound would then take some shots at the rim himself. If you hit the basket, you get the ball back. I always find the interaction of brothers on the basketball court so interesting. We seem to work so well together. There is so much mutual respect. There is so much camaraderie. I just love playing the sport, but now I have a new appreciation for it. Some of the same arguments that occur on the basketball court, if they were to occur five feet from it, would automatically escalate into a fight or a shoot out. It is as though in many instances, the basketball can serve as a safety zone. Nothing is absolutely, safe but the basketball court is a place where we try to get along with strangers. I'm not talking about tolerating someone, but actually working with someone who you have never met to accomplish a goal. Now if only we could bring that same friendship, teamwork and mutual respect we have for each other when we are playing basketball to our political, social and economic problems. Swoosh. "Good pass, Money." High five. Slam dunk. Good move. There it is.